The Destruction of Edingsville

Edisto Island's Wealthy 1800's Summer Village

Many interesting details included.

By: Sam Lybrand

Printed in the United States of America

ISBN-13: 978-1981368358

ISBN-10: 1981368353

10 9 8 7 6 5 4 3

EMPIRE PUBLISHING

www.empirebookpublishing.com

The picture on the title page was painted by Cecil Westcott as
he imagined what Edingsville looked like during the 1885 storm
that destroyed the "Village of Edingsville".

To the permanent residents of Edisto Beach and those visiting:

Edisto Beach is not the first popular beach destination on Edisto Island. Just up the beach, on the other side of Jeremy Inlet, there existed a highly sought after, wealthy beach village. It was called the "Village of Edingsville" or "The Bay," and was in existence during most of the 1800s.During its time it was the place to spend the summer. It had about 60 two-story plantation beach houses, two churches, a pool hall and even a hotel. Some say that a party atmosphere constantly existed in this village during the summer. Unfortunately, the hurricane of 1885 destroyed all of it in one wide sweep. There is now no evidence that it ever existed. Therefore Edisto Beach is not the first place where people came to enjoy the ocean off Edisto Island.

This is what this book is all about, the beginning and ending of Edingsville. Enjoy it and spread the word of its existence.

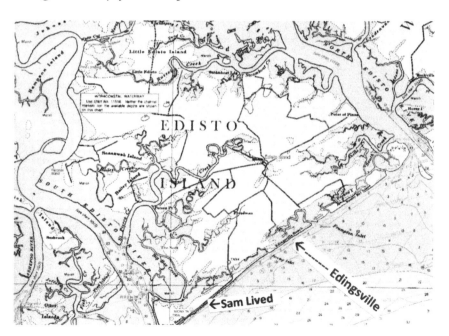

The illustration on the previous page is a general picture of Edisto Island. The arrow points to where Edingsville is located. Note that Frampton Inlet is to the north and Jeremy Inlet is to the south. It also shows where the North and South Edisto Rivers are located. Deveaux Bank is shown off the entrance to the North Edisto River. Deveaux Bank is much larger than shown on the map.

"The Lord gave, and the Lord hath taken away: blessed be the name of the Lord." Job 1:21 KJV

Be Alert!

Overnight or in a flash, life can throw curves at you and destroy your way of life.

Storms and fire can come upon you and destroy all that you have with little or no notice.

If you are not careful about who you associate with, some can turn on you without any notice.

Therefore you should constantly be alert of where you live and with whom you associate.

The people that built nice beach houses on Edingsville Beach did not take into consideration that they were building on a barrier island with no place to put a strong foundation other than sand.

This lack of consideration for what a hurricane can do to a building whose foundation was built on sand cost them the loss of everything they had invested in at Edingsville.

While they were having fun, they were not alert to what a hurricane could do to their beach houses. One hurricane made Edingsville only a memory.

Dedication

To all the past souls that settled Edisto Island and left such a rich history for all of us to read about. We can dream along with their dreams of how glorious and also how destructive life can be. Many lessons can be learned from the history of Edisto Island and its barrier islands.

Contents

Introduction

I'm an 80-year-old story teller with several ailments that come with age. It is my objective to get all I can find about Edingsville into book form before I get to the point where I cannot type and think clearly. Over the years I have read about Edingsville here and there, but I have never found all that is known about it in one place. This is my attempt to do just that --putting all I could find in one book for all to enjoy. It will be my attempt to write what I found in a fashion that will make you think you are sitting and listening to an old man telling you a story.

Again, this book is a consolidation of all I could find out about Edingsville so that anyone reading it would have a clear picture of what actually happened to Edingsville. The reason why what happened will also be clear to you after you have read this book from start to finish. My search for what happened lasted about a year and a half. After this time I just ran out of places to look for more information. I hope that you will find that I have covered the life of Edingsville from its beginning until a couple of hurricanes totally destroyed the "Village of Edingsville".

As a teenager I loved to drive up to the Pavilion and walk the beach in front of the State Park looking for fossils and ancient trash. I would walk all the way up the beach until I got to Jeremy Inlet. Sometimes, when the weather was warm, I would swim the Inlet and continue walking on Edingsville Beach looking for fossils. I was able to do this because my family was one of three families who lived on Edisto Beach full time during the late 1940s and early 1950s.

In the spring, there was a large colony of small terns nesting from where the State Park camp sites ended all the way to Jeremy Inlet. If you came near where they were nesting, a bunch of them would start bombarding you and making such a noise that you got out of there in a hurry. I'll tell you more about these terns and other sea birds in the separate section I have included at the end of this book on Deveaux Bank. Deveaux Bank is a new barrier island being built at the mouth of the North Edisto River.

At that time, Edingsville was only a narrow strip of land. The spring tides crossed over it and went into the marsh. The ocean keeps pushing this strip of land further and further inland. When the ocean had large waves, caused by the wind, it would pick up the sand on the ocean side and push it over into the marsh. My adventures on going over to what was left of Edingsville began my interest of what happened to it. I am now just getting around to doing what I have thought about all these many years. From time to time during my adult life I have gone over to Edingsville to see what I could see. I even took my girlfriend over to Edingsville for a picnic to ask her to marry me. Thankfully, she said yes.

Back then I observed two unique things that started my lifetime interest about this long narrow strip of land facing the ocean. There were large bricks here and there on the beach. I later learned that they were ballast bricks. I also learned that they were used to build cisterns under each beach house to hold rain water. I assume that these cisterns were also used as the foundation for each house. There were also large areas of hard black mud on the beach seen at low tide instead of sand as most beaches have. The mud was slippery to walk on so you had to stay clear of them. Seeing these two things would lead you to think, "Why are there large areas of mud exposed at low tide on the beach?" As my story unfolds, you will understand why there were large areas of hard black mud and many large bricks on the beach.

The format of this book is presented in sections of documents or books that related to Edingsville. When I use something, word for word, I will clearly identify it and put what I copied in italics

2

so that it will be clear that I copied the information. This book contains all the information I could find about Edingsville over a couple of years. It is my hope that compiling all the information I could find about Edingsville will tell the whole tragic story of "The Village of Edingsville" or, as some called it, "The Bay."

From time to time I will insert a **Rabbit Trail** with bits of information of interest but has nothing to do with the Edingsville story. But these **Rabbit Trails** do relate to this story somehow. These **Rabbit Trails** are my own words and what I think about whatever subject they deal with.

I am not including a table of contents so that you will read the whole story and enjoy it as you go along.

Oh, I am including some Bible verses at the beginning of each chapter to stimulate the reader's mind as to "How then shall we live?" **I'll put the answer to this at the end of this book. Look for it.**

So sit back and let me share with you all that I found out about one of my favorite places and what you can learn about building on a barrier island. Some of the information or bits of information will be repeated because I just liked the way it was written and how it sounded. Some people are just blessed with a pleasing way of saying things.

References

It is my attempt to write down what actually happened to Edingsville from its creation to when it was destroyed by several hurricanes. I have included a personal touch to make the story more interesting. I have searched the internet and many books on Edisto and found many different articles and stories written about Edingsville. Some I believe and some I wonder about. Many were written by people that have only recently visited Edisto and have only a limited amount of knowledge about this wondrous place. I have tried to set the record straight. As stated earlier, I have included several similar accounts of Edingsville because I liked the way the writers presented their tales about Edingsville and the language they used. Forgive me if I have left anything out or included the same thing too often. Remember I am an 80 year old and some things I do just don't make any sense. I guess when you get my age you can get by with a lot of things. My wife has edited this material. If something is spelled wrong or a comma or two is missing, call her. Most of the time I have no idea where commas go. What does a story teller need to know about commas?

Sources

*Rumbling of the Chariot Wheels – By: I. Jenkins Mikell (I believe I. Jenkins Mikell had the best way I have ever found of describing Edisto by his use of the English language.)

*Edisto Island 1663 to 1860 – By: Charles Spencer (I first met Charlie when I grew up on Edisto Beach in the 1940s. His father was our pastor at The Presbyterian Church on Edisto Island where I was a member, joining as a teenager. We were both members of the Cub Scouts run by his father. I also saw Charlie many times when he was on Edisto researching this book and visiting relatives here. Charlie's books are worth reading. I have not attempted to put as much detail in this book as Charlie has in his books. Again, I am just an old story teller.)

*Edisto Island 1861 to 2006 – By: Charles Spencer

*Edisto, A Sea Island Principality – By: Clara Childs Puckette (A little side line, Mrs. Puckette rode the school bus I drove in the school year 1954-1955. It is a small world.)

*Tales of Edisto – By: Nell S. Graydon

*Turn Backward O Time in Your Flight – A reminiscence of growing up on Edisto Island – by: Chalmers S. Murray (Chalmers Murray should be credited for all he has written about Edisto Island and particularly Edingsville. If it were not for him, much of Edisto's history would not have been recorded. His home place still exists on Frampton Creek. I recently visited his home place and it brought back memories of what I have read about him. I take my hat off to him. Oh, you can stand in front of his old home place and see the ocean breakers on the small strip of land that is all that is left of Edingsville. One day his front yard will be front beach if the ocean keeps pushing this small strip of land back toward his house on the creek.)

*Low country Hurricanes: By Walter Frazer, Jr. A series of descriptions of how people experienced hurricanes. Strangely, no dates were given.

*Carologue Magazine – "Memoirs of Federick Adolphus Porcher".

*The Charleston County Public Library: They also provided much of the material presented in this book.

*The Charleston County RMC: Also provided valuable information presented in this book. (It did help that the one in charge of the RMC is my first cousin, Charlie Lybrand. Thanks, Charlie!)

*Article found on the internet by John Burbage promoting his book— "Mr. Audubon, Mr. Beach and Bird Bank".

*The unpublished memoirs of Eberson Murray—Chalmers Murray's uncle. (These memories added a personal touch and are a valuable asset to this compiling of the story of Edingsville.)

*Article found on internet – "Lost … but not forgotten" by Donna York-Gilbert

*A portion of "More Tales of the South Carolina Low Country" by Nancy Rhyne with permission from John F. Blair, Publisher, www.blairpub.com

*An article found on the internet from a group that called themselves "Charleston Through an Artist's Eye." The article is titled "Edisto Island and Edingsville 1864". My interest is in an article written by Charlotte Forten. She taught freed slaves for two years on St. Helena Island and wrote about visiting Edingsville in 1864 along with a group of armed Northern soldiers.

*An article "Edingsville Beach; South Carolina's Antebellum Atlantis", by Nate Fulmer, MRD

*Archive: 1893 storm killed hundreds in S.C. – found on internet.

*Information from article found on internet titled: "Seabird Sanctuaries – Deveaux Bank" by South Carolina Department of Natural Resources.

As I stated earlier, some information about Edingsville is just common knowledge and often talked about in conversations about Edingsville.

*Mayor Jane Darby, who did research on the downward drift or current that if not checked, will help wash the beaches of Edisto's barrier islands away.

*Nate Fulmer who works for the Underwater Archaeologist, South Carolina Maritime Research Division told me that this downward drift or current had a name. It is called "Longshoredrift".

7

Chapter One

Historical Tragedies

"Be ye therefore perfect, even as your Father which is in heaven is perfect." **Matthew 5:48 KJV**

If you talk to anyone from any community, town or city about the makeup of where they live, some past or historical tragedy will come up in the conversation that is unique to that community. If you read a book or article about this community, more than likely it will have something about this tragedy. It may be only one paragraph long or several pages long. Each reference will give you a little different slant of the event to the point that many are really not sure what actually happened and how and why it happened. But this is their tragedy, and those who live in the community feel that they own this historical tragedy as their own.

We can learn from these tragedies by making sure the same thing does not happen to us. For example, it is not wise to build your home or community at the bottom of a large hill or mountain with very few trees on it. It may take a hundred years, but sooner or later a mudslide will come down this hill and probably wipe out what is built below it. Likewise, it is not wise to build on a floodplain. Soon or later the creek or river will overflow and destroy whatever is built on the floodplain. I know of a small creek that runs through a large subdivision that had a small floodplain. Builders built on this floodplain because they thought it unlikely that it would ever come out of its banks. Guess what? There was a very unusual wet month, and this creek had three hundred year floods that destroyed the houses the builders had built. This was not supposed to happen, but it did happen and should teach us a lesson to not build on or near any floodplain.

On our coasts, there are many barrier islands. A barrier island started out as a sandbar, maybe a thousand years ago. These barrier islands are made of pure sand and are vulnerable to northeasters or hurricanes. It may not happen in a lifetime, or maybe two or three lifetimes, but one day a hurricane is going to take out this barrier island, and nothing will stop it. Nowadays many people are building on the part of these barrier islands facing the ocean. An example of the danger people put themselves in when building in such locations is that the 1940 hurricane that hit Edisto Beach wiped out six blocks of front beach houses. The hurricane not only destroyed the houses, but it also washed away the sand that was the lot. The ocean came right up to the paved road going down the middle of the beach community. After the storm, there was no trace of these houses.

A story that is told over and over about the 1940 storm is that a man that owned a house further down the beach from those that washed away was about to leave the beach to get to high land when he remembered he had a new outboard motor that he had left on the porch. He went back to his house and moved the outboard motor from the porch into the house where he thought it would be safer. When he came back after the storm had passed, the porch was still there, but the house was gone.

"The Village of Edingsville" was built on the barrier island named Edingsville after the plantation in which it was included. It too was destroyed by one awful hurricane in 1885.

Edingsville is Edisto Island's tragedy.

If anything is written about Edisto Island, Edingsville's destruction is mentioned at least in a small part. As far as I can determine, every major book now in print about Edisto Island has something to say about the destruction of Edingsville. But none that I have found told the whole story. Therefore I hope to tell the whole story from its beginning until it was destroyed by an awful hurricane.

Chapter Two
Barrier Islands

"But whosoever shall deny me (Jesus Christ) before men, him
will I also deny before my Father which is in heaven."
Matthew 10:33 KJV

The story of Edingsville revolves around this Biblical parable.
As you read through this book keep this parable in mind. (Jesus
Christ is telling the parable.)

"Therefore whosoever heareth these sayings of mine and doeth
them, I will liken him unto a wise man, which built his house
upon a rock; and the rain descended, and the floods came, and the
wind blew, and beat upon that house and it fell not: for it was
founded upon a rock.

And every one that heareth these sayings of mine, and doeth
them not, shall be likened unto a **foolish man**, which built his
house **upon sand**: and the rain descended, and the flood came,
and the winds blew, and beat upon that house and it fell: and
great was the fall of it." **Matthew 7:24-27 KJV**

I sometimes wonder how many people really give any thought
to where the house they are getting ready to build or buy is
located.

The story of Edingsville could be wrapped up in a few words.
"The Village of Edingsville" was built upon sand!

A barrier island is a large sandbar that was built up over eons
of time and protects sea islands from the ravages of storms and
hurricanes. How this process began is one of nature's mysteries
that we will probably never know. Since these islands are made
totally of sand, they are vulnerable to any northeaster and

11

especially any hurricane. In a matter of a few hours, the ocean can destroy many yards of sand and anything in its path that is not securely anchored to something. But the problem is when you build on a barrier island there is nothing to anchor a foundation to except sand. The sand castle a child builds on the beach between the low and high water mark will be washed away with the first wave that hits it. Therefore there is no trace of the sand castle after the first wave washed it away. Likewise, any house built on the front beach of a barrier island is more than likely to be torn down by the surge of a forthcoming hurricane because it is anchored in sand and nothing else.

There is another factor that plays a part in the longevity of the barrier islands along the South Carolina coast. Everyone knows about the Gulf Stream and that it runs north. But few really understand that there is a southward current that runs near the coast. It is named "Longshoredrift". You will feel this current if you are swimming in the ocean off Edisto Beach or other barrier islands and realize that you are being taken south bit by bit. Before you know it, you will be several yards down from where you entered the ocean to swim.

As you read through this material, you will read references to the fact that Edingsville Beach was washing away by several storms. A northeaster will speed up this downward current and cause erosion to the beach. While living on Edisto Beach, I noticed all the erosion a northeaster caused. Sometimes yards of the beach would be taken away by a single northeaster.

As a reference, Edisto Island (a sea island.) has three barrier islands. They are Big Island (now called Edisto Beach) to the south, Edingsville in the center and Botany Bay to the north. Edingsville was the smallest, and for years it was considered worthless for farming because it was small and had nothing but big sand dunes running down the middle with jungle-like woods growing right behind the sand dunes.

One point of interest is that most plantation houses and churches built on a Sea Island, especially The Presbyterian Church on Edisto Island, have stood all the hurricanes that have hit them since they were built. The key is that there is stable soil to anchor these buildings. They were strongly built with wide outside walls using large studs with cross-timbers between the studs. The houses built on Edingsville were also built strongly, but they lacked a strong foundation and were thus vulnerable to being wiped out by a strong hurricane. The sand the foundations were built upon was just washed away like the sand castles children built on the beach.

For close to 60 years, during the 1800s, Edingsville was the place to be during the warm months of the year. But time caught up with it, and its turn came in 1885 when it was tested by a strong hurricane. It lost because all the buildings' foundations were anchored in sand.

Rabbit Trail: This has nothing to do with Edingsville, but as a child living on Edisto Beach, I used to climb up Mount Hope to view the rest of the beach. It was a sand dune located on Edisto Beach that was 65 feet above sea level and is still the highest point in Colleton County. Edisto Beach, also a barrier island, has to be constantly renourished to keep it from going the way of Edingsville. Left alone, there is no telling what Edisto Beach would look like today. The governing body of the Town of Edisto Beach has finally realized that there is a southern current that can cause erosion to the beach and have installed long structures out into the ocean to slow down this current and keep it from washing the beach away each time a northeaster comes calling. **Back to:**

The plantation owners either did not know about this current or if they did they ignored it and placed no importance to its destructive power. You might say that they did not have the equipment or ability to build structures out in the ocean to protect their beach houses. But the Romans built whole harbors using

13

rocks and some form of cement. Were our people during this time less smart than the Romans? Look what Governor Aiken did with Jehossee! The story goes that around 1860 he had one and a half million pounds of rice on hand and had 800 slaves. (Jehossee is another story worth telling. Maybe I'll work on Jehossee after I finish this book.)

Chapter Three

Edingsville

"Heaven and earth will pass away, but My words shall not pass away. (Jesus Christ speaking.)" **Matthew 24:35 KJV**

Just where is Edingsville located? What is left of it? Find Charleston, SC's harbor. The island facing the ocean to the south of Charleston Harbor is Morris Island; next to it is Folly Beach. Next is Stono River's ocean inlet. Next to it is Kiawah Island where all the rich people have their houses. Seabrook Island is next. Then comes the North Edisto River. Across the river from Seabrook Island is Botany Bay, Edisto Island's northern barrier island. Then you have Frampton Inlet which separates Botany Bay from Edingsville Beach.

Rabbit Trail: Up and down the South Carolina and Georgia coast you will find an island then a river or bay. Sometimes you find a large sound separating some islands. It is estimated that there are approximately 300 sea islands and barrier islands on the ocean side of South Carolina and Georgia. Over my lifetime I have been to many of these islands and crossed many of these rivers and bays. I can be a witness that God must have spent two more days after He had created the earth to create these beautiful islands and waterways. Get a safe boat and spend some time exploring this unique and beautiful area of America. Don't get a large boat because you might not be able to get into some of these waterways worth visiting. Oh, wear life preservers because Mother Nature can sometimes kick up her heels and make you wish you were on shore. **Back to:**

As I have mentioned, Edingsville is the barrier island just north of Edisto Beach (Big Island) and is separated from Edisto Beach by Jeremy Inlet. It has the Atlantic Ocean on the front, Jeremy Inlet on the south, Frampton Inlet on the north and the marsh area of Frampton Creek on the back of the Island. It is about a mile and a half long in a slight crescent shape. It is narrow and used to be less than a half a mile wide. Originally, it had high sand dunes in the middle with thick wooded areas behind the sand dunes. Before 1800 it was considered worthless for farming and only used as a place to go fishing or to camp out. It was not connected to any of the mainlands and was a true island. At the north end of the island was a boat landing. People would put in at Wilkinson's Landing (shown on the old map enclosed at the end of this chapter.) which is on the mainland on Frampton Creek. People used it to put in their boats and go over to Edingsville. Edingsville was also famous for a place to have a duel when someone insulted another and wanted satisfaction. The place was called the "The Sands." I have included a whole chapter on the "The Sands" later on in this book.

In this next section, I have listed what I found that people had to say about what Edingsville was like as it was being developed. In reading about Edingsville, there is some question as to whether it had sand dunes like Big Island has. These two comments verify that there were, in fact, large sand dunes on Edingsville.

An old timer stated: "There were **tall sand dunes** and a thick growth of trees on the little island. It was a wild but lovely place".

In Charles Spencer's book, "Edisto Island – 1663 to 1860" there was this comment: "The Episcopal chapel was consecrated in 1826 as St. Stephen's Chapel. It stood on a high dune near the center of the village."

I have included these two comments because they verify that Edingsville actually had high sand dunes and a heavy growth behind these dunes. A picture that I have enclosed further on in this book shows that Edingsville actually had sand dunes and heavy growth behind the sand dunes.

16

Therefore Edingsville was a long narrow barrier Island with large sand dunes down the middle and was of little use to the plantation owner until swamp fever became a real problem on Edisto Island.

Several articles I found mentioned that there were several cottages or small buildings some of the local people had built to stay in while they fished off Edingsville. I understand that there was a landing on Edingsville where fishermen could land their boats when they came over to the island. This landing was at the north end of Edingsville slightly inland on Frampton Creek. Wilkinson's Landing is still in use, and I personally have used it to go over to Edingsville to look for shells and fossils. One afternoon I took my girlfriend over to Edingsville in a canoe, putting in at Wilkinson's Landing. On the way back I sang to her. I still had it in those days! She later married me. Or as some say, "She took me in."

Rabbit Trail: Until recently I wondered how the old plantation owners built causeways or roads across marsh areas. If you know anything about coastal marsh areas, you will know that if you step on pluff mud, you will sink in very deeply. I found out that the way they built roads or causeways across marsh areas was called building **"floating roads or causeways."** The way they accomplished this was to place logs perpendicular, closely side by side, to the road being built and then place dirt or oyster shells on top of these logs. If the logs sank under the weight of the traffic crossing these roadways, they just placed more dirt or oyster shells on top of the logs. Some of these old roadways are still in use, and they still move with the weight of the traffic that goes over them. I bet if you really dug into these old roadways you would find them several feet thick. Back to:

The following was a map provided to me by U.S. Coast Survey, and I consider it to be the most important document found in this book. It shows what Edingsville's footprint looked like around

1850. It shows the complete island with dots for where houses were built, the causeway going out to the island and a clear picture of Frampton Inlet and Frampton Creek as they were at this time. It also shows Cowpens Island where the plantation owners kept their livestock while they were staying on Edingsville during the summer months. (Cowpens is the strip of high land located to the left middle of this picture next to the road going out to Edingsville.) Another feature that it shows is the boat landing that is still in use to this day. It is referred to as Wilkinson's Landing or Meads Landing. It is still used to get over to the strip of land that is left of Edingsville. When I get into the chapter on hurricanes, I will again use this map to explain where the footprint of the Village of Edingsville is presently located.

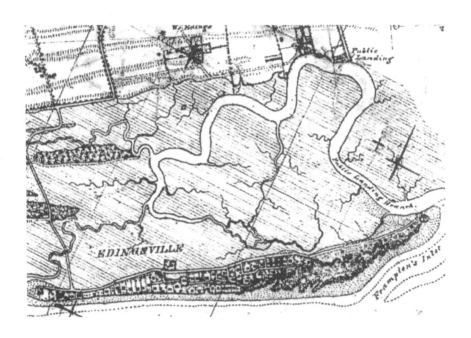

Chapter Four
The Solution

"The fool hath said in his heart,"There is no God." They are corrupt, they have done abominable works, there is none that doeth good." - **Psalm 14:1 KJV**

In the late 1700s swamp fever, also known as yellow fever and malaria became a real problem. The plantation owners did not know that mosquitoes were causing the fever, but they had figured out that if you could stay away from low swampy areas and ditches with water in them; you were less likely to get the fever. They also figured out if you could stay in places where there was a constant breeze you were also less likely to get the swamp fever. This was taken into consideration when deciding where to build. Most of the plantation homes were built on high bluffs where they got the breeze.

The Edings, who owned Edingsville, figured out what to do. Here is a bit of a larger article a friend of mine, Betsy Johnson, who lives in Charleston, SC, and is also interested in Edingsville, recently found. She was visiting the Carolina Room at the Charleston County Library and came across this article in a **Carologue Magazine. It was titled "Too good to last". By: Frederick Adolphus Porcher.**

Here is what I thought was interesting.

"Members of the Edings family, a prominent planter clan with deep roots on Edisto Island, took advantage of the escalation in building. The Edings arrived in South Carolina from Scotland in the late seventeenth century, and by the mid-nineteenth century, the family has amassed,' one of the largest and most valuable bodies of land on Edisto,' as an Edings descendent later wrote. Among the Edings holdings at various times were Seaside

Plantation (Also known as Locksley Hall), Bay View Plantation and a nearby barrier island upon which Joseph Edings seems to have started offering building lots for sale or lease as early as1800. The settlement that grew up on the island became known as Edingsville, and Williams Edings and John Evans Edings continued to develop it throughout the first half of the nineteenth century'" (Note the Edings family only leased lots on Edingsville.)

In the early 1800s, the Edings family, who owned Edingsville, came upon the idea of building a causeway across the marsh and a bridge to cross a small creek over to Edingsville. They then divided the island into lots and leased them to the plantation owners to build summer houses where there was a constant breeze off the ocean. Lots were leased over a long period of time, and the leases were recorded in the Charleston County RMC office. Three generations of the Edings family kept this leasing practice going. The names of three generations of Edings that leased these lots were Joseph Edings; his son, William Edings; and continued with his grandson, J. Evans Edings.

According to Charles Spencer, "By the Civil War, there were about fifty private homes, two chapels and a billiard parlor in the village, and at least another ten cottages or fishing shacks among the dunes between the village and Frampton's Inlet."

I obtained a list of the leases from the Charleston County RMC office. I have listed a sample of these leases in order of their Date of Deed. It would take several pages to list them all. The earliest transaction I found was 1801, and the latest was 1880. In my research, I came across written accounts that say these lots were bought from the Edings. But this proves that they were leased. Some of these recorded transactions were for various reasons. My point in presenting these transactions is to show that all dealings with lots on Edingsville were dealing with leases from the Edings family.

Record	Lessor	Lessee	Deed	Book	Page
7/29/1802	William Edings	Michah Jenkins	7/28/1801	E 7	75
2/29/1808	William Edings	Thomas Burden	8/9/1803	W 7	369
2/12/1806	William Edings	Joseph B. Seabrook	11/15/1805	R 7	112
3/5/1825	Joseph Edings	J Keith	2/12 1825	N 9	440
5/22/1834	Phoebe E Edings	William Edings Jr	1/21/1833	H 10	196
2/15/1844	William Edings	Thomas Lehre	2/14/1844	J 11	546
11/7/1847	William Edings	Benj S. Whaley	3/4/ 1846	S 10	348
4/17/1848	William Edings	Jno E. Rivers, Jr.	4/5/1848	A 12	219
2/12/1806	William Edings	Isaac J. Mikell	12/30/1852	T 12	517
7/23/1870	Joseph Edings	J.D. Geddings	7/23/1870	O 15	438
6/1/1874	Joseph Edings	William A. Boyle	5/22/1874	R 15	386
2/13/1875	Joseph Edings	William A Boyle	2/9/1875	R 15	407
6/17/1876	Joseph Edings	A. H. Heyward	6/1/1876	G 16	325
3/31/1880	Josephine Edings	Esther M. Seabrook	3/27/1880	H 18	15

A point of interest is that Charlie Lybrand, The Charleston County RMC, also sent me a copy of the actual document that was recorded by Joseph Baynard Seabrook in 1806 on page 112 of Book R 7. William Edings was the lessor. Note that this is the third transaction I have listed above. One thing that interests me was the transaction was done in British pounds. It is hard to read, but I believe the amount was twelve hundred and twenty-five pounds sterling. I am not sure what this would amount to in dollars at this time. At the beginning of the leasing, the lease amount was $30.00 for ten years. Three generations of Edings kept leasing these lots for approximately 88 years.

The next picture is a picture of the best layout I could find of how Edingsville was surveyed into lots. It shows the lots facing the marsh and the lots facing the ocean. It also shows the roads that were used to get to the individual lots where houses were built. Following this plat is a list of plantation owners or owners in general who leased these lots. This list is according to a survey made by White E. Gourdons, CE of the Village of Edingsville for J. E. Edings, July 1866. These people leased the lots numbered by their name. Note that this survey was done for the grandson, J.E. Edings. Also, note that some of the names listed by the surveyor seem to be spelled incorrectly.

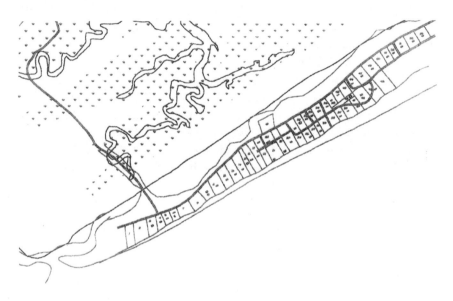

Lot#	Survey – Leased by	Lot#	Survey – Leased by
1	George Owens (Burnt)	27	Vacant
2	Vacant	28	Ephrain Bailey
3	M. Middleton	29	Edward Baynard
4	James Legare	30	Jno Wescoat
5	J Evans Edings	31	Jebez Westcoat
6	Sydney Legare	32	Edward Whaley
7	Vacant	33	Vacant
8	Dr. Bailey	34	Dr. James Whaley
9	Vacant	35	Vacant
10	J.E. Seabrook	36	Ephraine Seabrook
11	Rev. Wilson	37	E.W Seabrook
12	Hopkinson & Baynard	38	T.A. Baynard

13	Miss E.M. Whaley	39	Dr. R. Hannahan
14	Rev. William Johnson	40	J.J. Hannahan
15	Est. William Edings	41	Est. Jas. Hannahan
16	Theodore Becket	42	**Episcopal Church**
17	T.P. Mikell	43	Con Baily (burnt)
18	Jno. Wescoat	44	Col. Joe Jenkins
19	Mikele Seabrook	45	Mrs. W. B. Whaley
20	**Billard Saloon**	46	Mrs. Seabrook Jenkins
21	Miss E. Seabrook	47	W. Seabrook Jr.
22	W. E. Seabrook	48	Miss Minirva Street
23	Col. J. Whaley	49	**Presbyterian Church**
24	Maj. James Whaley V	50	Est. W. Murray (Burnt)
25	Hamilton Jenkins	51	A. J. Clark
26	L. R. Clark	52	John M. Jenkins

The interesting thing to me about this list of people is that they all could afford to build a substantial structure to use during the summer. These structures were built out of the best material available and were built to last. During this period Edisto Island and some of the surrounding plantations stood alone in that the plantation owners were rich beyond today's standards. Therefore they could afford to build such structures. Their wealth came from Sea Island cotton. Guess what? All this wealth came to an end as a result of the Civil War when the labor that grew this crop was taken away from them. Slaves were like tractors in that day. I guess these plantation owners, in all their wealth, just gave no thought about the possibility of hurricanes or even the loss of their slaves that did all the manual labor. So think about this list and all the wealth that came with them and then think about what it must have been for all this wealth to be taken away from them in a short period of time.

The following picture is a copy of an old painting, painted by Cecil Westcott which has been around for some time. It shows how Cecil Westcott, a local Edisto Island painter, thought the village of Edingsville looked from the ocean side of the village at a time when Edingsville was in its glory. All the houses were nice looking and well-built and provided all the comforts they had in their plantation houses on the mainland.

Note that all the houses had wooden siding like the plantation houses had. Several articles about Edingsville state that the houses were made of brick. Bricks of this quantity were not available during this period. If they had been made of brick, the beach would have been covered with brick after the 1885 hurricane.

Chapter Five
Life-Style

"The fear of the Lord is the beginning of knowledge: but fools despise wisdom and instruction." **Proverbs 1:7 KJV**

In this chapter, I have listed all the material I have found that tells about the lifestyle of the people that lived on Edingsville during the warm months. This chapter is to record what other people wrote about Edingsville in general and what I know living on Edisto Beach, just up the shoreline from Edingsville. When you get around a bunch of old-timers, stories of Edingsville often come up. Being interested in such things, I remember much of what was told about Edingsville. As you read these accounts, you begin to see how the lives of these people, who lived on Edingsville, were lived. Some of these inserts cover the same subject but in a different way. Collectively, you will begin to see how it was to live on Edingsville in its heyday. Each person that told a bit about the island looked at it differently. After putting all this together, I feel like I actually lived there in another life.

Here are the bits and pieces of what I know and what I found written about Edingsville. The source of each bit is clearly identified as to who wrote it and where it came from.

*A bit from Rumbling of the Chariot Wheels by I. Jenkins Mikell. (I could stop right here. This simple statement sums up the lifestyle of the people who spent the summers on Edingsville.)

"There the art of being busy and doing nothing was brought to a fine point by most of the younger planters."

The following is what I know about Edingsville from listening to old-timers, etc.

In general, the summer houses that were built on Edingsville were built out of the best material available. They were strongly built and finished on the inside like the plantation houses they were accustomed to during the colder months of the year.

I understand that they began building beach houses around 1800 and the real parties began around 1825 when enough families were spending their summers on Edingsville to begin having fun together.

When the weather began to get a little warm, about May first, a mass exit began to happen. Wagons were loaded with furniture and everything that the ladies felt they needed for comfort in their summer beach houses. The children even brought their doll furniture.

When they moved to their summer retreat, they even brought their horses and cows, which they put on a place they called "Cowpens." This was a strip of land that went out into the marsh with marsh on three sides. So all they had to do was close off the area that touched the land where the road to Edingsville began. This strip of land is shown on the map at the end of Chapter three of what the village looked like in the mid-1800s.

They even brought their hogs and let them run wild on the beach. Of course, they brought their chickens so that both chickens and hogs were readily available for slaughter when they were needed for the next meal or for food when they were entertaining. They lacked for nothing and sadly had slaves to carry out most of the hard work. What a life!!

Each house had a garden behind the house in order to have fresh vegetables. In addition, fresh produce was brought to the beach houses each morning, therefore they had fresh vegetables in ample amount. These gardens were planted in beach sand and had to be watered frequently because water just went through the sand. But surprisingly they had right nice gardens.

Rabbit Trail: When I was growing up on Edisto Beach, which is next to Edingsville, my mother also had a great garden in the beach sand. To help things grow, she would compost her kitchen scraps and till them back into her garden soil. From time to time she would hire a local boy from the island to help her with her garden. One of the boys that helped her called the process of putting my mother's kitchen scraps back into the garden soil, "Slopping the garden". **Back to:**

When everyone who was moving to Edingsville had gotten settled, the party began. There were many dances, picnics and about anything pleasurable you can think of. As you read about all that happened on Edingsville during the summer or warmer months, you will begin to understand that the houses they had built were only for sleeping and eating. When it was your time to have a party, then the individual houses were used as headquarters for the party.

Every morning the plantation owners would ride their horses to their plantations to see if their crops were being handled properly. He would also visit with the foreman in charge to make sure things were going as planned. He would make sure he got back to his beach house in order to have dinner at three PM. This seemed to be the main meal, and no one wanted to miss this spread. The plantation owners made sure they never were caught in the night air because they thought this was the main cause of swamp fever.

There was little or no swamp fever, as they called it because there was always a breeze on Edingsvile to keep the mosquitoes away. There were also no ditches or pools of water where the mosquitoes could raise their young. Therefore Edingsville beach was a pleasant place to spend the warm months of the year.

It seems that the young people had the time of their lives, fishing and gathering all kinds of seafood which was plentiful in

Frampton Creek. This creek ran behind Edingsville and also made it an island.

Wading in the surf was also a favorite pastime. The women and men did not bath together. The men were on one end of the beach, and the women used the other end. The women only waded in the surf and did not try to swim because it was thought that it was not ladylike for ladies to swim.

It is told that one of the boys had a herd of goats that were always eating in someone's garden and ganging up on the pet dogs. Another took his younger sister's baby carriage and made a land sailing sailboat, using an umbrella as his sail. He ended up in Frampton Inlet and got into much trouble with his parents. You can just imagine what a bunch of boys can get into when they had time on their hands with no real chores to keep them busy.

Rabbit Trail: It was well known that some of the Edisto plantation owners also owned houses in Charleston so they would have a place to stay during the "Social Season". It also was well known that the plantation owners, by building homes in Charleston, had an important role in developing the city. Therefore Charleston was developed from the outside in. After the hard work of the harvest, the plantation owners looked for excitement, and they found it in Charleston. Since this is a story in itself, I am not including a section on those plantation owners that owned houses in Charleston or where they stayed if they did not own a house in Charleston. This story is about Edingsville. **Back to:**

Since Edingsville was in a central location, it became the place to be for many years, beginning in the early 1800s. So much wealth that came together in such a small place created such a pleasant place that it became the place many people wanted to spend their summers.

*From Edisto – A Sea Island Principality by Clara Childs Puckette:

Rabbit Trail: Mrs. Puckette taught school in Adams Run and rode the school bus I drove during my senior year, the school year of 1954-1955. One day I looked in the rearview mirror and saw a book in flight and knew something was about to happen. Of all the places it could hit, it hit Mrs. Puckette in the head. I thought they had killed a teacher. But Mrs. Puckette just shook her head and said nothing. **Back to:**

"During those rich, wonderful years before war devastated the south and swept away the splendid life on Edisto, it seemed that no people knew so well how to enjoy life and get the most that was worthwhile and good out of this temporal, earthly experience. In winter they enjoyed the stimulating and pleasurable city life. In summer they relaxed at Edingsville, a most delightful beach, so conveniently near that the planters were able to go back and forth to their plantations each day. Produce from gardens was brought over fresh each morning to the beach dwellers. Edingsville was a lovely summer resort, not only for Edistonians, but also for other planters in the low country, especially well-to-do rice planters from neighboring areas, who were joking, of course, called it the 'Riviera of the Low Country.'

On the beach were to be found a church, peach orchards, and plum and fig trees in abundance, and large cisterns that provided plenty of fresh, pure water. ----- The main street ran along the edge of the marsh on the north side of the barrier island, and the lots ran south from it to the high tide level. All summer long the houses, most of them two-story places, were filled with guests. Edistonians, young and old, were a most sociable people and loved house parties and getting together.

Entertainment was not lacking at this pleasure resort. All water sports abounded. Healthful, happy, and busy, the summers passed, and sometimes there was excitement when, on moonlit nights, monstrous loggerhead turtles crawled out of the waves and up the strand to dig large, bottle-shaped holes above the high water mark, in which to deposit the prodigious number of their eggs. After covering the hole, these ancient creatures, so cumbersome on land, would lumber back to the sea and glide away."

*The following came from an unpublished article known as "Memoirs of Eberson Murray".

(I found it on the internet. I also found that it was widely used and quoted from an unpublished paper. The story of Edingsville would be lacking without Eberson Murray's account of what happened to Edingsville.)

"The topography of Edingsville Beach was much the same as that of other barrier islands of the South Carolina coast. Behind the big white sand dunes was a thick, impenetrable jungle of cassina, china-berry vines, honeysuckles, and yucca. The house lots were shaded by oaks and cedars. A fine laurel grew in Mr. Thomas Bailey's yard. People came from miles around to see the tree. It was the only one of its kind on the beach.

The dwellings were spaced far apart and stood in two long rows, one row overlooking the ocean, and the other the marshlands and creeks behind the island.

Although we had gardens in the village, most of our vegetables were brought down from the plantations. Many hogs were raised on the beach, for there they could run wild all over the place and feed where they pleased.

We boys had the time of our lives on Edingsville Beach. When we were not fishing, or eating raw palmetto cabbage (the heart of a palmetto tree) or sweet grass, or making bonfires, we were attending school, if the weather was not too hot and the surf not too tempting."

*The following is what Nell S. Graydon, in her book Tales of Edisto, had to say about Edingsville.

"Edingsville became a summer residence for Edisto planters early in the nineteenth century. William Seabrook had just bought his plantation on the Island from William Brisbane, who in the space of a few years had made an enormous fortune planting Sea Island cotton. So great were Seabrook's profits on this staple, he cleared the purchase price in two years, besides adding to his holdings of slaves. The other planters prospered similarly, and long before 1820, there were sixty large comfortable houses on Edingsville. Behind the houses were vegetable and flower gardens, carriage houses and slave quarters. Later, there were two churches and an academy. Edingsville was owned by the Edings family, and the land was leased to the other residents, usually for a period of ten years with the privilege of renewal, at an annual rent of four hundred dollars per lot.(Others say $300.00)

The planters, without knowing the reason, had discovered that the cool sea breezes brought relief from the dreaded 'country fever,' so prevalent in the Low Country during the hot months. Early in May, great activity could be seen in the big houses on the plantations as preparations were made to move to the 'Bay,' as Edingsville was often called. Wagons and carts loaded with house servants and necessary equipment moved over the burning sandy roads, with the owners following in their carriages.

Long summer days were spent swimming, sailing, dancing, giving teas, and entertaining friends from Charleston and the neighboring Sea Islands. For a few hours, each weekday the planters rode home to assure themselves that all was well with their crops, but they returned in time for three o'clock dinner. It was a leisurely, carefree life – in deep contrast to those years that followed the War Between the States."

*Charles Spencer had this to say in his book Edisto Island 1663-1860

"Cecil Westcott, who spent many summers at Edingsville as a youth and painted scenes of the village from memory later as an adult, told Murray (Chalmers Murray) that his family sat on their veranda on Sunday afternoons, enjoying the sea breezes and watching the 'afternoon parade.' I can shut my eyes now and see old gentlemen walking by, carrying gold-headed canes, young ladies in flowered muslins, arm-in-arm with their frock-coated escorts; old ladies out for an airing in their gleaming black carriages, and young men astride their prancing steeds.

Murray adds that 'the villagers seemed to spend the greater part of their time on the beach or in the churches, ballroom, or parlors of their neighbors.' For the young adults, there were 'riding parties, picnics under a grove of live oaks, surf bathing' and moonlight strolls along the beach. But 'mixed bathing was not permitted... The beach was divided into two sections, with a forbidden strand between. The young ladies would race to the eastern end of the island, and the men would make off in the opposite direction. The young ladies never attempted to swim, that would have been very masculine indeed, but contented themselves with bobbing up and down in the breakers.' and shrieking loudly for the fun of it."

Here is an interesting article I found on the internet. As I researched everything I could find about Edingsville, I was amazed at the way people described what they knew about the island. Each writer had his or her own slant. When you put all these stories together, you begin to know what went on at Edingsville and begin to think you could get up and go right down to there and enjoy all the fun.

*A portion of an article titled "Edingsville Beach: South Carolina's Antebellum Atlantis," By Nate Fulmer, MRD

"For those unaware, Edisto Beach was not the first popular vacation destination in that vicinity. During the first half of the

19th century, a different oceanfront settlement thrived just a few miles to the northeast on a narrow spit of sand between Jeremy Inlet and Botany Bay called Edingsville, or simply 'The Bay' by locals.

Established by and for wealthy island planters and Charleston families as a seasonal refuge from the stifling Low country heat and humidity and an escape from the malaria 'miasma' and mosquitoes of the marshes, Edingsville Beach was all the rage in the early 19th century. For a few decades at least, it was the place for the state's plantation elite to see and be seen. During this time, Edingsville hosted the largest concentration of plantation noblesse between Charleston and Savannah each summer.

Prior to development, the strand at Edingsville Beach was backed by an impressive wall of high sand dunes. The expanse of high ground behind the dunes was forested, but all that sand was otherwise worthless for agricultural use. The little island remained accessible by water until around 1800, when Benjamin Edings built a causeway from Edisto Island and began selling or leasing lots on the beach to local planter families.(Leasing, not selling.)

When Lafayette visited Edingsville Beach during his tour of America in 1825, his secretary Levausseur noted the 'altogether picturesque' appearance of the houses on the island resort."

Rabbit Trail: Did you know that Lafayette visited Edingsville? It is common knowledge that he visited the William Seabrook plantation and named one of their children. But it is not commonly known that Lafayette visited Edingsville. **Back to:**

"By this time, the seasonal community at Edingsville was well established, and it continued to grow into a thriving oceanfront vacation destination. In its heyday, there were several churches, a schoolhouse, a billiard saloon, and about 60 impressive brick and tabby homes. There were also a number of service buildings, fresh water cisterns, fishing shacks, and boathouses."

Another Rabbit Trail: I cannot find anywhere that the houses on Edingsville were built out of brick. If they were built out of brick, after the hurricane of 1885, the whole island would be covered with brick. It is my opinion that bricks in the quantity to build a house were not available during the time of Edingsville. **Back To:**

"Not unlike visitors to Edisto Beach today, summer residents of Edingsvile Beach probably spent very little time in their beach houses. Summer days at Edingsville revolved around outdoor recreation on the beach. At night, social functions ruled, with soirees and dances often rounding out the daily itinerary. But, like many popular fads, the good times at Edingsville Beach didn't last."

Here is another interesting article I came across on the internet. I thought it worth including. It gives another slant as to what Edingsville was all about.

*Lost.. But not forgotten by Donna York-Gilbert. (The author's feature on Edingsville Beach appeared in Charleston Magazine 2002 July/August issue under the title "Gone with the Wind")

"If there is ever a way to go back in time, the Old Edingsville Beach road can get you there. The road itself is seductive, mysterious, and hauntingly quiet, yet this road holds the secret to the past. The gnarled limbs of the old live oaks are dripping in Spanish Moss and leaning in as though they long to tell the stories of the past: the past that was filled with wealth, slavery, extravagance and tragedy; the past that resurrects itself with the ebb and flow of the tides washing up treasures along the shores of our own Jeremy Cay.

By the end of the 18th century, slavery and Sea Island cotton turned farmers into aristocrats in the backwoods of Edisto Island. The salinity of the Edisto Island marshes made rice planting difficult. The British stopped importing our indigo following the American Revolution, so the planters relied on the slaves to show them a West Indian way of growing another crop, cotton. And this was no ordinary cotton. Edisto's Sea Island cotton became the finest in the world, rivaling even Egyptian cotton. This king cotton was so fine; it was pre-sold at a premium years before the seed was planted. It is even said the Pope of Rome had his robes made from this silky, Protestant-born slave-harvested delicacy. This unique cotton and the high demand from around the world made the Edisto Island planters among the wealthiest planters around. And wealthy planters became the South's aristocracy.

The newfound royalty of Edisto plantation families married one another and ultimately connected the planters through blood and marriage. This unprecedented wealth allowed these families to own town-homes in Charleston and pursue other places of luxury and recreation... anything to escape the burdensome heat of those balmy Edisto summers.

Stifling heat, no breeze and abundant mosquitoes tarnished the charm of plantation life. Mosquitoes thrived in the farm-like environment of fields and stagnant ponds, and so did the fatal disease, malaria. It didn't take long before the Edisto gentry discovered a healthy retreat nearby called Edingsville Beach. The ocean breezes had a medicinal quality to them, and no one was dying of the dreaded diseases that plagued them inland on the plantations. Little did they know, but the breezy salt air kept the mosquitoes and their deadly malaria at bay.

Word spread rapidly about this tiny barrier island called Edingsville Beach. The Mikell family owned Edingsville Beach in the early 1800's. At one point, the Edings family owned the area and leased vacation lots to the planters as a summer respite. The plantation families built gracious, two-story, brick houses with sweeping verandas and fireplaces flanking both sides of each home. Elegant parties, regattas, horse races and elaborate banquets were the norm at this seaside resort for the Edisto principality.(According to paintings by Cecil Westcott houses on Edingsville were not built of brick.)

Each May, the Edisto planters would load their horse-drawn carts with the plantation furnishings and retreat to Edingsville Beach until the first frost of autumn. The men would return to the plantations each day to make sure all was in order, but would surely be back at the beach for the 3 o'clock dinner. Sounds of ladies laughing and splashing, men serenading their lovers, and echoes of sheer delight could be heard throughout the 19th century of Edingsville Beach.

In its heyday, there were at least 60 dwellings at Edingsville Beach. Among the summer homes was a schoolhouse for the boys to keep up their studies. There was an Episcopal and a Presbyterian church. And you can be sure there was a billiard saloon serving libations to all the God-fearing congregants along the shore. The Atlantic Hotel was built by the Edings family in 1852 and was advertised in the Charleston Courier as a 'salubrious Atlantic watering place.' Carriages, buggies, and saddle horses were available for the hotel guests. 'Seaside Surry' and 'Riviera of the Low Country' were other terms of endearments used to describe this playground for the rich. These were heady times for vacationers on the famed Edingsville Beach.

But like pages ripped from a great southern novel, the grandeur vanished and was literally gone with the wind. The War Between the States did little damage to Edingsville Beach, but it took a financial toll on the planters. It was a series of storms and hurricanes from 1881 to the turn of the century that extinguished Edingsville Beach. (See the last chapter for the actual dates of the hurricanes that destroyed Edingsville.) At the time, it sure seemed as though God was punishing the South and using nature's resources to wash away any evidence of her wealth and sins. There was no evidence left of Edingsville's golden era existence except for a tabby brick fireplace, broken trinkets, and mere memories of a magical time and place.

Like the legendary Atlantis, the 19th-century Edingsville is a memory of a once flourishing society buried at sea less than a mile from the shore of Jeremy Cay. And like Atlantis, this glorious village, with all its grandeur and extravagance, rests quietly, waiting to tell her story to anyone who will listen.

Today, if you are standing on the shore of Jeremy Cay, you may see remnants from those days roll up with the breaking of the waves. From china to slave's tools, or bricks from old mansions, Edingsville Beach sends whatever she can to remind us of her beauty and glory from another era.

The developers of Jeremy Cay have created a paradise from a slice of history. The lagoons, the pristine shells, the ancient fossils, and the abundant wildlife are rivaled only by the panoramic views and the brilliant rise and descent of the sun. The moon itself must favor Jeremy Cay, for it hovers so closely and luminously that even in the darkest hours, breathtaking sites are in full view. So as you gaze out at the whispering marsh grass or reflect on the sea's horizon, be ever so quiet and let the many ghosts of Edingsville bring her history back to the glistening shores of Jeremy Cay."

Commentary:

After reading these accounts of life on Edingsville in its heyday, one comes to the realization that life can be glorious but it also can be hard. One thing that comes to mind is that it appears that the plantation owners that built on Edingsville paid no attention to the fact that they were building on a barrier island with no place to put down a sound foundation. Sand and moving water just do not mix, especially when there is strong wind pushing the water. A cubic foot of salt water weighs approximately 64 pounds. A large wave can weigh thousands of pounds and when it hits something, what it hits is going to move and most likely be destroyed.

Edingsville dodged the bullet for a while, but in time, building on the front beach of a barrier island showed why that was not a good decision.

Note that Jeremy Cay is a fairly recent laid out gated community. Its entrance is just right of the entrance of Cowpens. It is located inland from where Edingsville once was. There is a long stand of marsh between it and the spit of land that is left of Edingsville. Since the land is low, all the houses are built on very high piling. The view from most of these houses is great in that you can see over the marsh to what was once Edingsville and to the sea in all its glory.

Rabbit Trail: I did not know until I began this project that there were three other places similar to Edingsville on the three other nearby islands. These were: Secessionville, located on a strip of land across the marsh from Folly Beach where plantation owners from James Island went during the summer. Likewise, Legareville, located at the junction of the Stono and Kiawah rivers, is where the plantation owners from Johns Island went for the summer season. Rockville, located on Bohicket Creek not far from the North Edisto River, was where the plantation owners from Wadmalaw went during the summer. **Back to:**

Chapter Six
Churches and Non-residential Buildings

"Poverty and shame shall be to him that refuseth instruction:
but he that regardeth reproof shall be honoured."
- Proverbs 13:18KJV

Schools

*The following came from an unpublished article known as "Memoirs of Eberson Murray". I found it on the internet. (He made two comments about the school in two separate places in his memoirs.)

"1).The village school was taught by Miss May Lee, a daughter of the Rev. States Lee, pastor of the island Presbyterian Church for over fifty years. It was a pay school, as I recall."

2).Our first free school was taught by Mr. Robert E. Seabrook, afterward principal of the Craft school in Charleston. The school was open in the summer season as well as in the fall and winter months. Teaching was generally a labor of love with Mr. Seabrook, for his salary was exceedingly small. He loved his boys and the whole community loved him."

Chapels, Billiard Parlor and Fishing Shacks

*Another quote from Charles Spencer
"By the Civil War there were about fifty private homes, two chapels and a billiard parlor in the village, and at least another ten cottages or fishing shacks among the dunes between the village and Frampton Inlet."

Churches

There were two summer churches built on Edingsville, Presbyterian and Episcopal.

*Here is what Charles Spencer had to say about these churches.

"The Presbyterians and Episcopalians were worshiping together once a week on Edingsville by 1821. They used an old dilapidated schoolhouse for a sanctuary, and the two ministers alternated Sundays, preaching and using their respective liturgies. 'Much harmony and kind feeling prevailed between the congregations.' In 1824 they jointly built themselves a real chapel on the beach, which they planned to continue sharing. But a serious disagreement arose about 'the internal arrangement of [sacramental furniture in] the building,' and unable to resolve it satisfactorily, the two congregations separated amicably. The Presbyterians sold their share in the new chapel to the Episcopalians and built themselves another chapel by the next summer. After this, they worshiped separately both on the island and on the beach.

The Episcopal chapel was consecrated in 1826 as St. Stephen's Chapel. It stood on a high dune near the center of the village and probably resembled the chapel in the drawing (painting in Chapter five). The Presbyterian chapel was on the back of the beach, near the marsh. Both chapels were moved to Edisto Island in the 1870s and were given, or sold to new African American congregations of their respective denominations."

*Comments from Eberson Murray's unpublished article

"There were two churches in Edingsville, a Presbyterian and an Episcopal. The Rev. William Johnson was rector of the Episcopal Church. Mr. Johnson worked hard to supplement the scanty salary given him. His people could afford to contribute very little.

I remember that he used to haul all his firewood in a little wagon on which he had rigged a sail. When the wind was right, he would hoist this sail and with his firewood aboard, would go skimming along the hard strand at a fine rate of speed. Mr. Johnson was not prosperous enough to own a horse or a mule. His sailing wagon was remembered many years after the old gentleman had passed away."

Rabbit Tail: Our family started going to the Presbyterian Church on Edisto Island in the mid-1940s. I officially joined it at age 13 or about 1950. Many times during this period we did not have a preacher, so we went to the Episcopal Church. In turn, when the Episcopal members did not have a preacher they came to our church. I guess nothing much had changed since the mid-1800s.

This has nothing to do with anything talked about in this book. But I would like it known that I sailed my bicycle also. I tied a long stick to the front of my bicycle handlebars, put a cross piece on the top of the stick, and tied a quarter of an old sheet to it. Then I tied strings to each corner of the bottom of the sheet and used them to adjust the sail as the wind changed directions. Away I would go toward the pavilion. You would be surprised how fast the wind would push a bicycle with this small a sail. So Mr. Johnson had nothing on me.

Store

*Charles Spencer had this to say in his book Edisto Island 1663to 1860

"There was also a small store on the beach, but its location has not been found on the map. Boys went to school in the summer each morning, but were free to play in the afternoon; there was no school for girls. To a child, 'life on Edingsville seemed a long happy holiday.' Fishing, riding and swimming were their main sports."

Hotel

*From article Lost... But Not Forgotten, by Donna York-Gilbert

"**The Atlantic Hotel** was built by the Edings family in 1852 and was advertised in the Charleston Courier as a 'salubrious Atlantic watering place.' Carriages, buggies and saddle horses were available for the hotel guests. 'Seaside Surry' and 'Riviera of the Low Country' were other terms of endearment used to describe this playground for the rich. These were heady times for vacationers on the famed Edingsville Beach."

The following is an ad for the Hotel, talked about in the bit above on Edingsville provided by the Charleston County Library. It does not have a date. I found it interesting, and it verifies that Edingsville actually had a hotel.

ATLANTIC HOTEL ON EDINGSVILLE, EDISTO ISLAND

"The subscriber takes this method to inform the traveling community and the public generally, that the above new ESTABLISHMENT will be opened for the reception of visitors on the 1st of August.

A rare opportunity is now offered to those in search of health and pleasure, to avail themselves of the benefits of this salubrious Atlantic Watering Place.

Situated upon the seaboard, free from the influence of the country atmosphere, it combines all the attractions of a healthy Bathing resort.

Carriages, Buggies, and Saddle Horses, for both sexes, to enjoy the excursions on the ocean beach, and suitable conveyance for visitors and their baggage to and from the steamer Etiwan, always in readiness. Engaged now, by application to the subscriber, by mail, on Edisto." - E.S. Mikell

Here is another sort of strange ad in the paper that was provided by the Charleston County Library dealing with the hotel. I have not been able to confirm if this hotel ever opened. Here is how it was presented.

A CARD

"The subscriber begs to announce to his friends and the public, that the occurrence of unavoidable circumstances, sickness of servants, etc, compels him, as a duty to himself and the public, to delay the opening of the Hotel on Edings Bay, to the 1st of August, ensuing. This indulgence, he feels satisfied, will more than compensate those disappointed, by enabling them to enjoy many improvements."- E.S. Mikell

Chapter Seven
The Sands

"Righteousness exalts a nation, but sin is a reproach to any people." **Proverbs 14:34 KJV**

The area at the end of Edingsville next to Frampton Inlet was called **"The Sands."** There were no houses in this area and was where the original landing was for people to get to Edingsville to fish before the causeway was put in. It was commonly known that this area was used for duels.

In this era of time, you had better not insult someone or someone's family member. If you did, it was almost certain that a duel would take place to keep one's honor. You just did not insult someone or call them something insulting. **Duels were mostly held by the top echelon of people** so that they would maintain their status in their society. Duels were more common in the lower southern part of the nation in rich places such as Edisto Island. Duels were generally stopped after the Civil War because many thought that enough killing had taken place.

As I stated, many duels took place on the sands. I looked hard, and I only found the record of one duel. I am sure there were others, but I could find no record of them. One of the best known was between a Mr. Bailey and some smart acting guy from England. This account of a duel is found in several places, but I chose to use the account found in I. Jenkins Mikell's book, **Rumbling of the Chariot Wheels**. I like his style of writing and his word usage. I recommend that anyone interested in the history of this era read this book. He covered many subjects not found anywhere else.

"Would that there were none but bloodless duels for me to record, but alas! The 'Sands' claimed its fair share of tragedies in the death of more than one principal in these 'affairs of honor.' To mention one only that has come down to us. The Gilland-Bailey affair. Tradition is to this effect. Mr. Gilland was reputed to be an expert marksman in the use of a pistol. Could at every shot 'snuff a candle'—the accepted test of a dead-shot man. His sang froid was all that could be desired in a 'principal.' A disagreement arose between Mr. Bailey and himself, as in most of these cases trivial at first but soon leading up to an exchange of cards, then a challenge. It required a courage of no mean sort to stand before a man of such skill-you not possessing it-it meant sure death, so far as probabilities went. There was only one kind of courage that was greater, and very few men possessed it, the courage to refuse to fight. Mr. Bailey's friends insisted that he should somewhat familiarize himself with the handling of the pistol so far as limited time would allow for practice. It was known he 'could not hit a barn door,' a little practice enabled him to 'hit the door;' and no more; and on that, he ventured on the field believing and feeling he would be the victim. At sunrise on the appointed day he made preparation looking to the end. With his surgeon, his second and a few friends, he started at dawn for the 'Sands;' he had also conveyed a mattress upon which his body, perhaps lifeless, could repose on the sad march homeward. His adversary passed him on the way and noted the preparation for the return of the body. He himself felt no necessity for sure preparations.

On arriving, after the customary courtesies, of the extremist kind, had been exchanged, and preliminaries arranged, Mr. Bailey's second, in handing him his weapon, remarked in a lowered voice, 'Your chance is to fire on the word;' bowed, then stepped back. For an instant there was the stillness of death; then a clear inquiry rang out 'Gentlemen, are you ready'? A pause; 'Fire'—'On the word,' a shot rang out—a fraction of a second, another. Mr. Gillland was seen to quiver, stagger, then sink to the ground. With a dilatoriness born of absolute confidence, his aim was too deliberate, his fire too delayed. He had received his death wound. The 'unnecessary' mattress served a purpose never thought of in the first instance, it acted as his resting place on the journey home.

His body lies in the cemetery of the Presbyterian Church, Edisto Island. On the stone over his grave, we now can barely decipher

Arthur Alfred Gilland
Born in London, England 1811
Died February 12, 1839
'Prepare to meet thy God.'

The following tradition has come down to us. He was staying in or visiting Charleston. In an hour of exuberance of spirit among his companions at some gathering, he planned a visit to Edisto Island, saying to them, 'I will wake these people up; meet at supper, to which I invite you all, on my return, when I will exhibit some mementos of my trip.'

The 'waking up' business began, and ended in his encounter with Mr. Bailey."

*A portion of what I found on the internet by Reddit, Inc. about dueling.

"By the 19th Century dueling was mostly practiced in the southern part of the country, and for some at least, continued to be a part of aristocratic life right up until the Civil War, which can be viewed as its essential and point. There are a few records of duels being held in the years afterwards, but they are with much less frequency, and by the 1880s, the laws of the various states, which previously had allowed for comparative slaps-on-the-wrist, were finally quite harsh, with step punishment for merely planning a duel and the death penalty for killing your opponent. In South Carolina at least, the change in the laws was finally pushed through after the 'Cash-Shannon' duel in 1880, which saw Col. Shannon killed by Col. Cash in-front of a crowd of several hundred people, and covered nation-wide-the New York Times called it a murder even. The event certainly helped to drive home the reality of dueling, no doubt assisted by the 14 fatherless children left behind by the victim (this, of course, exempts the 'Wild West,' which I don't really deal with, so I can't comment on what the truth is there.)"

*Here is another explanation of dueling by Chris Hutcheson and Brett McKay I found on the internet.

"In our modern age, solving a problem by asking a dude to step outside is generally considered an immature, low-class thing to do.

But for many centuries, challenging another man to a duel was not only considered a pinnacle of honor but was a practice reserved for the upper-class, those deemed by society to be true gentlemen.

'A man may shoot the man who invades his character, as he may shoot him who attempts to break into his house.' - Samuel Johnson

While dueling may seem barbaric to modern men, it was a ritual that made sense in a society in which the preservation of male honor was absolutely paramount. A man's honor was the most central aspect of his identity, and thus its reputation had to be kept untarnished by any means necessary. Duels, which were sometimes attended by hundreds of people, were a way for men to publicly prove their courage and manliness. In such a society, the court could offer a gentleman no real justice; the matter had to be resolved with the shedding of blood."

In my opinion, there were other duals held on "The Sands," but I could not find a record of them. I guess that a duel was something that was not a thing to be talked about and recorded.

Chapter Eight
Ghost Stories

"The wicked flee when no man pursueth: but the righteous are bold as a lion." - **Proverbs 28:1 KJV**

Edingsville has left behind several ghost stories. When you have such a tragedy as the destruction of the Village of Edingsville, you are bound to have some ghost stories that get larger and more mysterious as the years go by. My children loved to go on camping trips and hear ghost stories around a campfire at night. The following are some ghost stories that I discovered as I searched for material about Edingsville. Who really knows if they are true or not and where the stories originally came from.

*This material is excerpted from More Tales of the South Carolina Low Country by Nancy Rhyne. It is used with permission from John F. Blair, Publisher, www.blairpub.com
"The Ghost of Edingsville Beach"
By: Nancy Rhyne

"In the days prior to the Civil War, when Edisto Island planters become millionaires from the production of Sea Island cotton, they built and maintained beach houses on Edingsville Beach, across a tidal creek from Edisto Island. Edingsville Beach had a wide, sandy beach, where conchs, whelks, cockles, and other fabulous seashells washed up with each tide. The houses of the planters faced the sea, and they all had the same architecture. They were all two-story, had a brick chimney on each end, many windows, and a house-length porch on the beach side.

It was during this time that Mary Clark, a daughter of one of the wealthy planters, become engaged to Captain Fickling. The engagement was no surprise to Edisto Islanders, for both Mary and her fiancé were descendants of old island families, and they had been childhood sweethearts. So no expense was spared as plans for the wedding were made. Finally, the wedding day was at hand, and the bride, on the arm of her father, walked under a canopy of native vegetation, which included green myrtle branches and water spider orchids, as she made her way down the aisle of St. Stephen's Church. When the bride and groom were pronounced man and wife, they left the church and stood in the churchyard to receive the guests as they exited the sanctuary of St. Stephen's. They invited their guests to a feast that was then being spread on long tables set up on the beach. Plantation cooks had been working all night and all that day on the platters of food. The cooks used recipes that had been handed down for generations. The wedding was the talk of the island.

Four weeks after the wedding, the groom set sail for the West Indies, and the bride began to look forward to his return almost before his ship was out of sight. It was October, and most of the planter families were still in residence in their beach homes. It was customary to not leave until after the first frost in the fall season.

Each evening, just before sunset, Mary Fickling walked down to the water's edge. She looked out over the cold water and thought of her husband, far from home. On the evening of October 12th, the rolls and swells of the sea began to build, and Mary began to worry about her husband. She knew that his return was overdue, and if an October hurricane was churning the sea, his ship could be involved. There were no warnings for such storms then, but somewhere deep inside her, she felt that a dreadful hurricane was indeed coming. When she returned home, she found others were also worried about a hurricane. Someone said that the causeway to the mainland was already flooded and any crossing was out of the question.

Within minutes, the hurricane hit Edingsville. The house in which Mary was staying trembled and swayed, and the structure started to give way. As members sat scared and quietly, they listened. First, there was great sucking of air, and then there was total darkness as sea water washed into the house.

For Mary and others, it was a long night of terror as they struggled to stay alive. Morning brought an eerie calm, and the rise of the sun brought a scene that would never be forgotten. Trees were lying everywhere. Some beach houses lay askew with porches, chimneys or windows washed away. Heavy pieces of furniture, chairs, and sofas were scattered along the beach. As Mary was looking over the beach in disbelief, she spotted a dark, lumpy form floating in the sea. As she stood compelled to watching this form as it washed closer toward the shore, she saw that it was the form of a man. She ran into the water, and as the form got closer to her, she recognized the body of her husband. With a shuddering cry, she got down into the water and with tears streaming from her eyes, embraced his lifeless body in her arms. Mary was to learn later that his ship was indeed in the middle of the hurricane and that his ship and all hands were lost at sea."

There are no beach houses now where Edingsville was located and no reminders of the days when this place was a fabulous resort. Over the decades this beach has been tormented by devilish hurricanes and unusually high tides. What remains today is no more than a sliver of sandy beach adjacent to a marsh.

The story goes… it is said that on moonlit nights a young girl can be seen running into the waves and pulling the form of a man upon its shore. This is the ghost of Edingsville Beach."

* I found this conversation by an old man tucked away in some old papers.

In thinking about Edingsville, all the pretty two-story beach houses are now gone. The high sand dunes and beautiful oaks have been washed away. The Sunday parades of all the ladies and dressed up men marching up and down the beach are gone. All is gone except a narrow strip of land that the surf swallows every now and then.

Standing on this narrow strip of land at high tide you can hear strange sounds, but there are no bands. During the Civil War Yankee soldiers stationed on Edingsville gave concerts for the local people. I guess it was so peaceful for them they never wanted to go, and their souls just stayed and did their thing.

Then there was the image of a beautiful lady that walked the beach in the moonlight. If you stand still and let your mind wander, you can see this lady in the yellow streams of moonlight.

* Another story told by an old man that is worth telling:

A while back three boys who were walking down the beach near sundown noticed a black object between two small sand hills. Upon investigating, they discovered that what they had first thought was a clump of seaweed was human hair black as jet and lying around a bleached skull. In a few minutes, the complete skeleton of a women was unearthed, and the boys ran home to inform the older folks of the gruesome find. The villagers reached the conclusion that it was the frame of a women lost at sea in some hurricane. This discovery, the Negroes believed, 'put bad mouth' on the beach, and soon the word went out that 'de bay is haunted.'

Three men walking near the spot where the skeleton was found saw the figure of a woman dressed in white, walking towards the surf. It was a moonlight night, and the men thought they recognized the woman's features. This lady had become restless as was her habit and had decided to set out on the beach and make a short walk before retiring. They said nothing to the lady and kept a good distance to the rear. On and on the woman walked, and once in a while she would pause and glance over her left shoulder. Her feet came nearer and nearer the water, and when she reached the glistening strand, hesitated a split second, and then with firm tread, walked into the breakers and disappeared from sight before the men could attempt a rescue.

Terrified, the trio ran as fast as they could to the village and gave the alarm. They were greatly taken aback, however, when they found that the lady, who they could have almost sworn had just a few minutes ago committed suicide by drowning, was very much alive and in the best of spirits. She had not left the house that day for any purpose. The mystery was never solved, and the men stuck to their story.

Chapter Nine
The Civil War

"For to him that is joined to all the living there is hope: for a living dog is better than a dead lion." - **Ecclesiastes 9:4 KJV**

Edisto's plantation owners were ordered to evacuate Edisto Island at the beginning of the Civil War. According to what I can find out, by word of mouth, because I could find only a few records of where they went, the Islanders went to several places in South Carolina and even into Georgia and rode out the war. There is one record of where the Edisto residents went during the Civil War. Uncle Eberson Murray recorded this statement in his unpublished Memories, "With the exception of a few years spent in Yorkville and Mabinton, SC., during the Confederate War, and brief interludes in Beaufort and Charleston, Mr. Murray has lived his entire life on Edisto." Therefore Edingsville's summer homes were left vacant during the war. I did find an account of where Rev. States Lee evacuated to Edgefield County near Aiken, SC.

*An article written by Charlotte Forton who taught freed slaves on St. Helena Island in 1864. The article is about a sightseeing visit she had to Edingsville with some armed Northern soldiers.

"Early in June, before the summer heat had become unendurable, we made a pleasant excursion to Edisto Island. We left St. Helena village in the morning, dined on one of the gunboats stationed near our island, and in the afternoon proceeded to Edisto in two row-boats. There were six of us, besides an officer and the boats' crews, who were armed with guns and cutlasses. There was no actual danger; but as we were going into enemy's country, we thought it wisest to guard against surprises.

After a delightful row, we reached the island near sunset, landing at a place called Edingsville, which was a favorite summer resort with the aristocracy of Edisto. I found a fine beach several miles in length. Along the beach, there is a row of houses, which must once have been very desirable dwellings but have now a desolate, dismantled look. The sailors explored the beach for some distance, and returned, reporting 'all quiet, and nobody to be seen'; so we walked on, feeling quite safe, stopping here and there to gather the beautiful tiny shells which were buried deep in the sands.

We took supper in a room of one of the deserted houses, using for seats some old bureau-drawers turned edgewise. Afterward, we sat on the piazza, watching the lightning playing from a low black cloud over a sky flushed with sunset, and listening to the merry songs of the sailors who occupied the next house. They had built a large fire the cheerful glow of which shone through the windows, and we could see them dancing evidently in great glee. Later, we had another walk on the beach, in the lovely moonlight. It was very quiet then. The deep stillness was broken only by the low, musical murmur of the waves. The moon shone bright and clear over the deserted houses and gardens and gave them a still wilder and more desolate look. We went within-doors for the night unwillingly.

Having, of course, no beds, we made ourselves as comfortable as we could on the floor, with boat-cushions, blankets, and shawls. No fear of Rebels disturbed us. There was but one road by which they could get to us, and on that, a watch was kept, and in case of their approach, we knew we should have ample time to get to the boats and make our escape. So, despite the mosquitoes, we had a sound night's sleep.

The next morning we took the boats again and followed the course of the most winding of little creeks. In and out, in and out, the boats went. Sometimes it seemed as if we were going into the very heart of the woods, and through the deep silence, we half expected to hear the sound of a Rebel. The banks were over-hung with a thick tangle of shrubs and bushes, which threatened to catch our boats, as we passed close beneath their branches. In some places, the stream was so narrow that we ran aground, and then the men had to get out, and drag and pull with all their might before we could get clear again.

After a row full of excitement and pleasure, we reached our place of destination, - the Edings Plantation, whether some of the freedmen had preceded us in their search for corn. It must once have been a beautiful place. The grounds were laid out with great taste and filled with fig trees, among which we noticed particularly the oleander, laden with deep rose-hued and deliciously fragrant flowers. And the magnolia, with its wonderful, large blossoms, which shone dazzlingly while among the dark leaves. We explored the house, -- after it had first been examined by our guard, to see that no foes lurked there, -- but found nothing but heaps of rubbish, an old bedstead, and a bathing-tub, of which we afterward made good use.

When we returned to the shore, we found that the tide had gone out, and between us and the boats lay a tract of marsh-land, which would have been impossible to cross without a wetting. The gentlemen determined on wading. But what were we to do? In this dilemma, somebody suggested the bathing-tub, a suggestion which was eagerly seized upon. We were placed in it, one at a time, borne aloft in triumph on the shoulders of four stout sailors, and safely deposited in the boat. But through a mistake, the tub was not sent back for two of the ladies, and they were brought over on the crossed hands of two of the sailors, in the carry a-lady-to-London' style.

Again we rowed through the windings of the creek, then out into the open sea, among the white, exhilarating breakers, - reaching the gun-boat, dined again with its hospitable officers, and then returning to our island, which we reached after nightfall, feeling thoroughly tired, but well pleased with our excursion.

From what we saw of Edisto, however, we did not like it better than our own island, (St. Helena) except, of course, the beach, but we are told that farther in the interior it is much more beautiful. The freed people, who left it at the time of its evacuation, think it the loveliest place in the world, and long to return. When we were going, Miss T. – the much-loved and untiring friend and physician of the people-asked some whom we met if we should give their love to Edisto. 'Oh, yes, yes, Miss!' they said. 'Ah. Edisto a beautiful city!' And when we came back, they inquired eagerly. – 'How you like Edisto? How Edisto stan?' Only the fear of again falling into the hands of the 'Secesh' prevents them from returning to their much-loved home.

Ah! Edisto, a beautiful city! Yes. Indeed, she is!"

Commentary:

I used this article because it described the result of the evacuation of Edisto at the beginning of the Civil War. All the plantation houses, including the ones on Edingsville, were left vacant and unattended. This must have been an awful time for the plantation owners that had put so much work into building profitable plantations.

The creek she talks about is Frampton Creek. Today it still winds around with many little creeks running off it. There is still a landing on Frampton Creek that has been used for many years. Frampton Creek goes beyond the causeway that now goes to Jeremy Cay and I can see how a rowboat could follow it to the front of the old Edings plantation house. The plantation is now called "Seaside Plantation." The present owner is about my age and was part of our group coming up. I can remember her lying on the front of my sailboat sunbathing as we sailed all over Big Bay Creek and St. Helena Sound. Life was fun coming up on

Edisto Island. This article brought about memories of places I was familiar with in my teen years.

Chapter Ten
Buildings Moved from Edingsville to Mainland

"If My people, which are called by My name, shall humble themselves, and pray, and seek My face and turn from their wicked ways; then I will hear from heaven, and will forgive their sin, and will heal their land." - **2 Chronicles 7:14 KJV**

After the Civil War, several Edingsville buildings were moved to different places on the mainland of Edisto Island. I have included the information on one of these buildings. What amazes me is that people in the 1800s could move entire buildings using only oxen and logs. Some were taken apart, board by board, and rebuilt on the main part of Edisto Island. The following is a description of the moving of one such building.

*I found this information about Bailey's Store on the internet. It came from South Carolina Department of Archives and History.

"Bailey's Store has significance as one of the last, if not the last, surviving commercial buildings on Edisto Island from the nineteenth century. It is thought that this building was built before 1825 on Edingsville Beach, a popular antebellum seaside resort off Edisto Island, and moved to its present location ca 1870, in reaction to that beach's abandonment during the Civil War. Thus, it is one of the very few pre-war relics from Edingsville, for all remaining structures were swept into the ocean in the hurricanes of 1885 and 1893. The building was moved in two parts to Store Creek, and placed together again, to be used in connection with a gin house already on that location. Bailey's Store is a two-story, weatherboarding clad, rectangular, side-gabled roof building which at one time faced 180 degrees in the opposite direction, but when Highway 174 was moved about 1940 (1936-1937), was turned around. For many years the Edisto Island Post Office was located in a one-story shed roof addition on the south elevation, which has recently been removed. A hipped roof covering extends from the western elevation, suspended over the front door. The fenestration of the façade is asymmetrical and is composed of three bays on the first story and five bays on the second story. There is also a one-story, hipped roof addition at the rear. Listed in the National Register November 28, 1986."

Some say that the building was floated down some creeks and pulled by yokes of oxen with logs to roll the building to its present location. Can you even imagine moving a building in the way they moved things in the 1800s?

Rabbit Trail: My wife and I live about a mile and a half down Store Creek toward the South Edisto River. As a child living on Edisto, I remember going to buy things from Mr. Hunter who ran a general store in this building.

The thing that that has stuck with me the most is that if my daddy wanted to buy 10 gallons of gas, Mr. Hunter would go to a tall pump with a glass container up top with gallons marked on it. He would hold a large lever and pump ten gallons into the glass container. He would then put a long hose attached to the pump with a faucet at the end into the car's gas tank and release the gas into my daddy's car.

I also remember getting mail from the old Post Office that was attached to this building. The mail carrier was Billy Hills (William Seabrook Hills). I married his daughter, Joyce. Therefore I have been connected to this old building from my youth. Back to:

Here is a little paragraph from the Annual Tour of the Edisto Island Historic Preservation Society booklet about the moving of the present Zion Reformed Episcopal Church from Edingsville.

"In 1890, Henry W. Bailey donated funds to buy land across the road three hundred yards south of Trinity Church. Some historians believe that the church on that property today had been Trinity's gift of St. Stephen's Chapel from Edingsville Beach, moved there and reconstructed. St. Stephen's Chapel dated from 1826."(Note the 1890 date does not make a lot of sense because the 1885 hurricane destroyed most of Edingsville. But the 1826 date is more reasonable. I have included this because I believe it is true that it was moved from Edingsville to its present site.)

Chapter Eleven

What really happened to "The Village of Edingsville"?

"If we say that we have no sin, we are deceiving ourselves, and the truth is not in us." - **1 John 1:8 KJV**

What really happened to Edingsville? There are several things or events that caused the destruction of the most fun-loving place on earth to be no more. One thing that had a lot to do with the destruction of Edingsville was that the beach houses were built on a barrier island with no place to put a sound foundation. When the waves and wind came, they just washed these houses away. The storm that destroyed these houses did not destroy, the houses on Edisto Island proper because they were built on sound foundations.

The Civil War had something to do with the destruction of Edingsville in that the houses were left vacant for many years and were not kept up or even occupied. But this really did not play a great role in Edingsville's destruction because the houses were strongly built with the best timbers available at the time.

Beginning in the mid-1800s, Edingsville began to wash because of normal occurrences of the spring tides and northeasters. As a teenager, I noticed that the ocean was constantly cutting away at the shoreline in front of our house on Edisto Beach. This is just normal activity for the shoreline of any barrier island. Edisto Beach is constantly fighting the ocean because of natural ebb and flow. But the plantation owners did not seem to be bothered by this constant washing or did not have anything to combat it with. I guess they were too busy having fun, so they did not worry about such things.

All kinds of dates are given for the storms and hurricanes that hit Edingsville, but the following are the hurricanes I can verify. Poor Edingsville seemed to be constantly bothered by hurricanes.

A small hurricane that hit in 1854 did some damage but not enough to really worry the Edingsville dwellers. In fact, the story goes that several houses were damaged and were removed from Edingsville around this time.

Between 1854 and the big one in 1885, three more hurricanes made landfall on Edingsville. They were the hurricanes of 1874, 1878 and 1881.

Then came the big one. Out of the blue came the hurricane of 1885 that completely destroyed all but two or three of the houses on Edingsville.   A little further on I have included Uncle Eberson Murray's account of experiencing this horrible storm. I have to assume that it took out many of the tall sand dunes to be able to take out the houses built on the marsh front.

Other than the warning Mother Nature gives of approaching storms, hurricanes just showed up without any warning. People that lived in the 1800s did not have the luxury of the forecasts we now have. I believe that if they had not been partying all the time, they would have noticed that the air was getting thick and that the sea was about to show her ugly side.

To add insult to injury the worst hurricane to ever hit this area was the hurricane of 1893. In its march up the coast, it is reported that it killed around 1000 people, 33 on Edisto. Of course, it is reported that it helped destroy the remaining sand dunes. Some say it left some remnants of these once beautiful sand dunes.

The hurricanes of 1911 finished the job and only left a long narrow strip of land. The footprint of "The Village of Edingsville" is now way out in the ocean. Just for information, no other hurricane hit this area until the 1940 storm that damaged much of Edisto Beach.

The rest of what is presented in this chapter are bits and pieces of information that relate to the destruction of Edingsville.

Before I start with what I found about the hurricanes that helped destroy Edingsville, I'd like to give you a few facts for your information about living on the coast. If you live on the Gulf coast or the east coast of The United States, you are going to have to deal with hurricanes. So take notice of these facts. The Good Lord gives a person plenty of warning of the coming of a hurricane, even without modern communication. The first thing a person should take notice of if a hurricane is approaching is that the birds will be the first to go inland. If you go to the beach and find no sea birds, you'd better take notice. The next thing that will happen is large swells will begin to hit the beach, and they will be far apart. A hurricane is like a barge going through the water. It pushes up water or waves in front of it, and they show up a long distance ahead of it in the form of large sea swells. So when you see large swells begin to hit the beach a long time apart, take notice and consider leaving for high land. Then you will notice all the clouds racing in one direction toward the center of the storm. When you see clouds racing you had better have already made your plans to head for high land. The last thing you will see is all the palmetto limbs going in one direction. When you see this, you'd better be looking out a window at them from a sturdy house upon a high bluff.

Rabbit Trail: Now let me tell you something from my own experience. In the fall of 1947, in time to enroll in the Edisto Island Grammar School, we moved to Edisto Beach after spending all the summers there since 1942. We had not been there very long before we were advised by the police that a hurricane was going to hit Edisto Beach and to get off the beach ASAP. We were invited to ride the hurricane out in the Hopkinson's plantation house on School House Creek, a small branch of Store Creek. It was morning when we arrived at the Hopkinson's house. Not long after we arrived, the wind started blowing, and the tide began coming in at an unusually high rate of speed. My father became concerned that we might be in trouble from rising water. The sound of the wind was something I had never experienced before. It was unworldly and just downright scary. After a time (I'm not sure how long as I was only 10 years old.) the wind stopped, the birds came out, the sky was blue, and everything seemed calm. We thought the hurricane was over. But not long afterward, the wind began from the other direction and seemed like it was blowing harder. The wind sucked the creek almost dry. We then realized that the eye of the hurricane had just gone over us. I'll never forget the weird and frightening sounds the hurricane winds made as it passed over us. Since we were in a well-built old plantation house, the hurricane did no damage to it. It just put small limbs all over the yard. **Back to:**

*A portion of an article titled "Edingsville Beach: South Carolina's Antebellum Atlantis, By Nate Fulmer, MRD

"As opposed to the sudden storied destruction of Atlantis, it was an extended series of unfortunate events that led to the loss of this once-famous settlement by the sea. Almost as quickly as the village of Edingsville Beach rose to fashion, unstoppable forces of nature intervened and began to take the whole island and everything built on it right into the ocean.

Soon after seasonal occupation at Edingsville Beach began, visitors noted that ever-lapping tides and shifting sands were taking a toll on the once-expansive beach. Around twenty of the island's houses were lost to the angry Atlantic surf before the first shots of the Civil War were fired just up the coast in Charleston. The island was largely uninhabited during the War Between the States, but the erosion continued, unaffected by the human conflict in which the resort's residents were embroiled.

By the time the War of the Rebellion was over, around 40 houses, two church buildings and the billiard saloon were still standing. Of course, the devastation of the southern plantations' economy left most Low Country planters bankrupt, and many of the founding families were forced to abandon their summer homes forever. In the decades following the war, some of the beach houses were leased by African-American farmers and sharecroppers. Recognizing the impending loss to the mighty Atlantic, at least one merchant dismantled his store into sections in order to float it several miles inland to higher ground. By 1872, storm surges and tidal action had greatly undermined the natural sand dune barriers that protected many of the homes from the ocean. At this point, a vicious cycle of erosion and neglect began to claim the remaining structures in rapid succession.

The knockout blow to the historic occupation at Edingsville came in August of 1885, in the form of yet another direct hit by a hurricane. Eberson Murray was present when the storm struck and was horrified to witness the surge strip the porches from his and his neighbors' houses. According to his account, he watched helplessly as the surge continued to grow and the high tide came in. By nightfall, his house and the other oceanfront homes had been swept away into the Atlantic. Only a couple of houses remained standing after that storm, and those last bastions of civilization on the island rapidly fell into further disrepair. Abandoned altogether after the 1885 storm, the infamous Sea Island Hurricane of 1893 erased the final vestiges of the settlement of Edingsville Beach once and for all."

As I have talked about earlier, a barrier Island has no defense against a hurricane. When you think that a cubic foot of salt water weighs about 64 pounds and that a surge in front of a hurricane maybe 20 feet high and several miles across, then there is nothing that it will not tear down when it comes ashore. The Village of Edingsville was built on the sand of a barrier island. Therefore when the great hurricane of 1885 hit, there was no defense. The great wall of water that came ashore in 1885 with hurricane force winds behind it just wiped out everything in its path. When it was over only a few torn up houses were left. The following is the account I found about this tragedy.

*From Eberson Murray's unpublished article.

"When the **storm of 1885 broke**, I was working up on the island, about five miles from Edingsville. Becoming alarmed about my people, I shut up shop and made my way to Edingsville on foot, through a raging gale. How I ever lived through the bombardment of falling tree limbs, I do not know to this day. It was only by a miracle that my brains were not knocked out.

At last, I reached the village. The spectacle that met my eyes made me fear at once for the safety of the settlement. The high tide that morning, driven by a tremendous gale, had carried away the porch of our house and had undermined the foundation. Members of my family were hastily moving our furniture to a house on the back beach. Our next door neighbor had also lost his porch. The water was swirling around our feet, and the worst was yet to come for the wind was increasing in velocity and another tide racing in.

We had moved just in time. The water rose higher and higher, and that night both of the front beach houses collapsed. Mr. E.A. Bailey's and ours. This was the end of the village of Edingsville. No one dared to live on the barrier island after that terrible experience.

He continued: The **storm of 1893 came** on us while we were in church. By the time services were over, it was blowing such a gale that I decided to spend the night with a relative who lived near the church, rather than run the risk of walking home – a distance of about five miles. My brother, Chalmers, was marooned on the northern end of the island, and my mother and sister were alone in the house at Seaside.

The next morning after the storm had subsided, I left Cypress Trees plantation, and made my way home by slow stages. I was very anxious about my mother and sister, and it seemed that the journey lasted months. The highway was impassable on account of fallen trees, and I was forced to go out across fields in order to make any progress. All of the low places were flooded, and several times I sank to my waist in water. What had once been fields white with Sea Island cotton were now desolate wastes of salt water, already giving off an unpleasant odor of decaying vegetable matter.

Upon reaching Saint Pierre's Creek, I was horrified to find that the bridge was gone. There was nothing to do but to make a wide detour through Sea Cloud plantation. I walked two miles out of my way through sticky, evil-smelling mud, and at last, saw our house standing against the grey sky. My mother and sister had been terrified at the onslaught of the wind and the rushing tide but seemed none the worse for the experience. My brother arrived soon after I came home, worn out and dispirited. He had stopped at his store on the way down and found that all of the merchandise was ruined with salt water, and the building badly battered.

Our dwelling had weathered the gale and would not need any great repairs, but all of the Negro tenant houses were gone, the poultry drowned and the entire cotton crop destroyed. It was a dreary scene – marsh sedge deposited all over the yard, trees stripped bare of leaves, and mud plastered over the landscape.

Thirty-one Negroes had been drowned on the island that night. It was the worst storm that Edisto Island had ever experienced."

A bit from a book I came across on the internet titled: Low country Hurricanes by Walter Fraser, Jr. As far as I could determine, it is a selection of accounts of storms or hurricanes. It did not give dates. I just liked the way he presented his writings.

"The storm moved north toward Charleston, littering the marsh with small craft. Edingsville Island, facing the open sea and frequently pounded by hurricanes, took the brunt of the storm. By early Saturday evening, a howling east wind had driven the tide high up on the beach; the waves crashed under the few remaining summer homes. The terrified occupants fled to the house of D.A. Stevens, considered to be the only safe structure on the Island. The sea undermined, and the wind blew over three houses. A correspondent there wrote 'The existence of Edingsville as a village has now ended ... nothing remains to remind us of its former glory except a few dilapidated houses.'"

Another saying by Fraser in his book:

"Edisto Island residents watched what some said was one of the most terrifying hurricanes ever known. It 'Burst' on them on Thursday night, and the following morning the ocean surged across Edingsville Island. The sea rushed under the piazzas of several houses on Edingsville, and residents concluded that this vulnerable strip of sand was no longer safe as a Summer Resort for thirty-six houses. The storm raged, felling trees, destroying fences and bridges, and flattening the cotton crop on Edisto. Three-quarters of the crop was declared lost. Edingsville was so inundated by the hurricane that planters finally abandoned the once lovely summer resort. It was to be reclaimed by the sea."

*From Chalmers Murray's Turn Backward O Time In Your Flight.

"The last houses in the village of Edingsville were swept away in the hurricane of 1893, and no one dared to rebuild. It is impossible to mark out the place where the village stood, for the site is under water now."

A little more from this book:

"I will never forget my first sight of the ocean. My father had
rowed the family over to Edingsville Beach, the site of a little
village which, years before, had been wiped out by a series of
hurricanes. The breakers there were probably no more than two
feet high but, to me, they seemed the height of mountains. They
frightened me so much that I ran back up the beach as fast as my
feet could move and I refused even to go wading. I think my
father, dressed in an old pair of pants, went into the surf and
seemed to enjoy it thoroughly. Ina only shut her eyes and started
to cry. It must have been at least two years afterward that I
ventured to put my feet in the ocean.

In those days there were tall sand dunes and a heavy growth of
trees on the little island. It was a wild but lovely place. Now all of
the dunes and trees have been washed away, leaving only a
narrow strip of sand which is covered by water during spring
tides. At one time sixty dwellings, a schoolhouse, a saloon and two
churches stood on the strand. Erosion has exposed old creek beds,
and fishing now is a poor sport."

Still a little more from this book: This is about the storm of
1911. It is believed that the hurricane of 1911 took out the rest of
the sand dunes and trees left on Edingsville and left only a narrow
strip of land. It is as if during any storm the ocean took a large
shovel and took the sand on the ocean side and threw it over into
the marsh, thus moving the small strip of land further and further
from where the footprint of the original village was. I have
included a picture of Edingsville that was supposed to be taken
before the 1911 hurricane. But I am not sure. The 1893 storm was a
terrible storm and could have taken out the rest of the sand dunes
and the rest of the trees left by the 1885 storm. What this picture
does show and confirms is that there were sand dunes and heavy
tree growth on Edingsville at one time. The picture is located on

the page after the account of the 1911 hurricane. Note that the house talked about in the next bit is located on a high bluff on Frampton Creek and overlooks the marsh side of Edingsville. I have recently visited this house, and it is in good repair. From the porch of the house, you can see across the marsh to the narrow strip of land that is now all that is left of Edingsville. I believe that if the ocean keeps pushing the sand of this strip of land back over the marsh, one day the land side of Frampton Creek will be the front beach.

"The hurricane of 1911 was the first severe storm that I remember. It came up on a Sunday just as we were getting ready for church, so we had to call off the trip. I watched grey, dishrag clouds scurry across the sky and felt the house tremble with the wind, which had by then reached gale force.

My father went outside for several minutes and came back shaking his head. If the wind kept up, it would be the end of the cotton crop, he said. He shook his head again. "I'm afraid that will mean that you can't go back to the Citadel," he told me. I thought he was talking through his hat. Somehow, the Murray family always managed to come through every crisis. My father (up to now) had always been good for a loan.

The wind was making a weird sound; sometimes it whistled, sometimes it roared, and sometimes it howled. The house seemed to be doing a kind of dance. I looked out at the creek and marsh in front. In a little time, all of the marsh was covered with water, and I could see breakers rolling in. My mother managed to cook some kind of dinner on the kerosene stove. The wood was too damp for a wood fire.

My father went upstairs and returned with a dazed look on his face. "The minute I opened the parlor door, all of the window panes crashed," he said. 'I'm afraid all the panes upstairs have been broken. We will have to spend the night down here,"

Ina started to cry, and nothing my mother could do would comfort her. The wind was now blowing higher than ever, and I expected to see the roof fly off but, despite my fears, this did not happen. The howling gale kept up all day and all night. My mother had made a bed on the floor, and I lay down with the rest, but I couldn't sleep for a long time. Ina, however, went to sleep almost at once. I think my parents caught cat naps.

Monday dawned at last, but the heavy rain clouds obscured the sun. My father remarked that, luckily, the hurricane had struck at low tide. Otherwise, the yard would have been flooded. He looked out and saw that the cotton had been stripped from the bolls and lay in white patches in the fields. What had been a promising crop had been completely destroyed. But I didn't worry very much. I fully expected that the money would be raised so that I could continue my schooling at the Citadel. I should have been thoroughly ashamed of myself. I had flunked my freshman year and had been 'permitted to retire' before the school year was out because of the demerits I had acquired, though I was allowed to enroll for the next year, which was 1912.

The house must have been very sturdy since we did not lose our roof; only many windows were smashed. The barn and buggy house and stable escaped with only minor injury. This was rather remarkable since the wind was estimated to have reached one hundred miles an hour. A tramp steamer was blown ashore on Botany Beach but, as I recall, no lives were lost.

Though the wind was still high, I went upstairs to my room and fell asleep immediately. When I awoke the next morning, the wind had died down, and the sun was shining. When I returned to the Citadel (My father had borrowed the necessary money against next year's crop), I wrote an essay on the hurricane for which I got a high mark.

Rabbit Trail: The 1885 hurricane was bad enough, but 1886 brought another earth-shaking event. A strong earthquake hit the

Charleston area in 1886. Local lore tells that the earth rippled on Edisto Island and the earth even opened up in several places. The following is Uncle Eberson's account of how he and some of his cousins experienced the earthquake. **Back to:**

*Here is Uncle Eberson Murray's account of the Earthquake.

"The earthquake of 1886 made a deep impression upon me. I had gone over to Toogoodoo, across the river, to visit some nieces and cousins. We had hardly settled ourselves on a bench just outside of my cousin, Tosa King's house, when the first shock came. The girls crowded me and held me in a suffocating grip. If the earth had opened as we had expected, we would have been swallowed up in one mass of struggling, squirming humanity, for there was no getting us apart.

When the thundering subterranean sound had ceased, we could hear the Negroes at prayer meeting screaming in terrified voices, 'Oh, Lord, judgment done come, better pray hard you sinners.'

In less than fifteen minutes we saw a red glare in the northern sky, indicating that fire had broken out in Charleston. We heard afterward that lamps had been knocked over by the earth tremors, setting parts of the city on fire.

The second shock brought Cousin Tosa's chimney down with a crash. We sat close together the rest of the night, waiting for the morning. For months afterwards we would jump whenever we heard the sound of thunder."

*Article found on the internet titled: Archive: 1893 storm killed hundreds in SC. By: Joey Holleman

"The 1893 storm took much the same route as was predicted from Floyd, hugging the Florida coast before the eye came ashore near Beaufort. Remember the picture of boats stacked on top of each other in the tidal creeks after Hugo? After the 1893 storm, the creek banks were piled with bodies. Nobody knows exactly how many died--at least 1,400, maybe 1,500, and possibly 2,000. To this day, it ranks as the third deadliest hurricane in North American history. The storm had no official name. Officials hadn't started giving these monsters names and human characteristics at that point. If they had, this one would have been angry, strong and, worst of all, stealthy."

Note: There is a book written by Bill and Fran Marscher titled **The Great Sea Island Storm of 1893. It tells all about the 1893** storm in detail. If you want to learn all about what this great storm did to the Sea Islands around Edisto, then get a copy and read it. This storm did great damage to Edisto and killed many people also.

Edisto's Historical Tragedy:

For about 50 +/-years the plantation owners of Edisto Island had the time of their lives getting away from the mosquitoes during the warm months of the year. It seems that they gave no thought that they had built lovely two-story beach houses on sand which had no defense against high tides caused by northeasters and hurricanes. Three hurricanes utterly destroyed this happy place, and now there is nothing to show that there was once a village of happy people on the now little strip of land called Edingsville Beach.

The hurricane of 1885 came ashore with little or no notice and destroyed all but a few of these lovely houses and took out some of the sand dunes. The Hurricane of 1893, which is said to be the worst hurricane to hit the Atlantic coast in recorded history, took out the remaining houses and just about all of the sand dunes. The hurricane of 1911 took out the remaining sand dunes and left only a small strip of land that the spring tides go over into the marsh as if there was no land there at all.

The footprint of the village houses is now way out in the ocean, and the ocean keeps pushing the small strip of land further and further into the marsh. One day, if the ocean continues to push this strip of land back, the river bank of Frampton Creek will be the front beach.

On the present beach, there are patches of hard black mud that once was a marsh. These mud patches show that the ocean has pushed the small strip of land that is left over the marsh. You will also find old bricks on the beach that were once part of the cisterns and foundations.

What a tragedy! All that fun has gone into the history books and especially in the tales of local people telling about what happened. As generations pass, the stories of Edingsville get dimmer and soon no one will be talking about this 19th-century oceanfront resort. Therefore the reason I wrote this book is because I spent many happy hours on this tiny beach as a teenager looking for fossils. Since this little strip of land was special to me, I want to keep it alive in Edisto's history. At low tide, you can see the piling (way out in the ocean) from the old bridge that was once a part of the causeway going over to Edingsville. It seems that hurricanes would just not stop washing away the island from the start and finally completely took it off the map. 1885 was the year that took away one the most pleasant places on earth.

.

On the following, pages are photographs and drawings that show different aspects of Edingsville.

The first picture shows what Edingsville looked like in the 1850s with a white line showing approximately where the shore line is now (2017). This drawing was provided by Nate Fulmer of the SC Maritime Research Division.

This picture shows torn down sand dunes with the forest behind it. The carriage dates the photo.

The picture on the next page is also a dated. The interest here is how high the sand dunes on Edingsville were. Provided by Gretchen Smith of the Edisto Island Historic Preservation Society.

The picture below is a copy of a painting by Cecil Westcott. It shows his interpretation of what Edingsville looked like in its

prime. Provided by Gretchen Smith of the Edisto Island Historic Preservation Society.

This picture shows what is left of Edingsville Beach. There is nothing left but a narrow strip of land that high tides cross into the marsh. The ocean keeps pushing this strip of land further and further back inland. The footprint of the original village is now way out in the ocean. Looking at this picture, one would never know that once there was a lively village of plantation beach houses built around tall sand dunes that were washed away by hurricanes. (This picture came from a group of pictures found on the internet.)

Chapter Twelve
Reflections

"And this gospel of the kingdom shall be preached in all the world for a witness unto all nations; and then shall the end come."
Matthew 24:14 KJV

A favorite cousin of mine, Jann Poston, whose family has lived on Edisto for generations, gave me a fictional children's book about a little girl that lived in the 1950s near Edingsville. The book is about her dreaming of going out to Edingsville and playing with children of that time. This little children's book started to make me think a little deeper about what it really took to create or build this seaside village.

This book brought back childhood memories of living on Edisto Beach as a child. I used to love to lay back on a grassy spot and look at the clouds and wonder about what could be. With this little book in mind, I began to let my mind wonder about what life was actually like on Edingsville in about 1800 (or so) when it was in its heyday.

I let my mind wander and imagined myself on the Edisto Beach side of Jeremy Inlet looking over at Edingsville to see what was going on. The first thing I saw was an image of many people building the causeway over to Edingsville. It seemed to me that most of the people were slaves with a foreman supervising the whole operation. It was quite a task building a causeway across all that mud and marsh grass.

I looked a little further, and I saw several surveyors laying out the lots and marking where the roads were to go. I wondered how they were going to get lines across the tall sand dunes and through all that jungle behind the sand dunes. I assumed that they came over to Edingsville, putting in at Wilkinson's Landing and rowing over to do their work.

As I stood there with my mind wandering, I saw people riding horses across the causeway that had now been finished. They were going about picking out the lots they wanted to lease to begin building their summer beach houses. The lots on the ocean side seem to go first.

I heard all kinds of activity going on over to my left and realized that many people were involved in cutting out studs for the summer houses and others were sawing out long planks for the sidings and floors. This was no small task. Others were gathering old bricks for cisterns and foundations. As I looked across Jeremy Inlet, I saw in my mind a flurry of activity going on to build the summer resort for the plantation families to escape to in order to avoid getting swamp fever.

As I stood there looking across Jeremy Inlet, I could see in my mind what was going to become "The Village of Edingsville." I realized that lines on a drawing were more than just lines. These lines represented many people's creative abilities and many hours of hard work.

About this time a few laughing gulls landed in the inlet near me and made such a noise that I came to my senses, and in my mind, I started walking back toward the State Park where my car was parked, as I had done many times before. As I walked back toward my car, I came back to reality. From time to time I still have in my mind how Edingsville was established and how it was destroyed by vicious storms that took away a beautiful place.

The people that spent the summers on Edingsville experienced a level of enjoyment that we will never get the opportunity to experience. They had extreme wealth and were able to do what they wanted to do and servants (slaves) to do their bidding. I do not condone slavery, but that was reality back then. Just think what it would have been like to have someone fix your meals and for you to party until daylight.

WHAT A LIFE! We can agree with this kind of life, or we can disagree with the way it was. But in any case, there was a "Village of Edingsville," and this book is a record of its existence. In my case, I still like to sit and dream about such a place.

Now I have said all I want to say about Edingsville and put together all I could find about this seaside village. I hope you have enjoyed all that I have put together.

Creation of a Barrier Island

Deveaux Bank

"He that hath the Son hath life, and he that hath not the Son of God hath not life." - **1 John 5:12KJV**

As far back as my teenage years, I have been interested in Deveaux Bank. As a teenager I often went over to Rockville, SC, to participate in the annual summer sailboat races. I raced in the Lighting Class and enjoyed every moment of each race. Rockville is on Bohicket Creek, across the North Edisto River from Edisto Island. I loved trying to get the best of the boats I was racing against. Oh, to be a teenager again, making my sailboat skim across the water without a sound but the slapping of the water against the hull of my boat. What a life for a teenager!

Rockville is the place where the oldest continuous sailboat race party in America is held. If the weather were calm enough, we would leave our dock on Big Bay Creek, and tow my sailboat with a small motor boat to Rockville. We would travel in the ocean in front of Edisto Beach and Edingsville and continue through an opening between Botany Bay and Deveaux Bank. Going through this opening, you could see all the birds that were nesting on Deveaux Bank. The pelicans were particularly obvious because there were so many.

Of course, if the weather was bad we had to take the long way around, using the Inland Waterway.

Therefore this chapter is a **Rabbit Trail** and has nothing to do with the destruction of Edingsville. But it shows how barrier islands are formed and their vulnerability to the whims of the ocean. The formation of Deveaux Bank is a good example of this. The ocean and the wind created Deveaux Bank, and they can destroy it. As a young person living on the ocean, I was interested in such things and observed Mother Nature's use of the ocean to build and to destroy. At an early age, I learned to respect the ocean and its creeks because you did not get a second chance if you capsized in a storm. The point is you don't go out in storms. If you see a storm coming, you get ashore as soon as possible. If you do get caught in a storm, you need to get the center of gravity as low as you can in the boat. You keep your bow into the waves and never let yourself get parallel to the waves because the wave will throw you out of the boat. You then head for the nearest land and ride the storm out.

The entrance of the North Edisto River is shallow and has always had many sandbars as far back as records show. The reason is that the North Edisto River is not a river that goes far inland as the South Edisto River does. Therefore there is not the strong current or large volume of water that goes into the sea from far inland that would keep the mouth of the North Edisto River deep and open. Thus the North Edisto River is really a sound like the many sounds between all the sea islands from just north of Charleston to the Florida Coast.

There is a record that a navigator named Andrew Deveaux helped the British troops in the 1700s navigate the entrance of the North Edisto River, land on Seabrook Island and go across the land to attack Charleston, SC during the Revolutionary War. Therefore the barrier island named Deveaux Bank was named for him. Actually, it should be called Deveaux Banks because from time to time there are many banks at the entrance of the North Edisto River you have to be aware of.

My first job out of the service took me away from the Island. Shortly after my family got settled, I took them down to Edisto Beach to visit my parents. While I was there, I decided to take a walk on the beach in front of the State Park down to Jeremy Inlet, like I had done many times as a youth. While walking down the beach, I had the feeling that something was missing. I soon realized that the terns were not there and had stopped nesting there. I knew about Deveaux Bank from passing it many times going to Rockville. I thought to myself that Deveaux Bank would be a good place for my birds.

I got busy and ordered all the old navigation plats of the entrance of the North Edisto River as far back as I could. I found that Deveaux Bank came out of the water in 1910 as a sandbar and began to get bigger and bigger. I also saw that it was never attached to anyone's property. Thus it did not belong to anyone. I then contacted the State Government and asked that they give it to me so I could build fences on it to grow it bigger and bigger for my birds. I communicated with the State for about a year until the government official in charge of this decision to **keep it in reserve for the people of South Carolina**. In other words, the State did exactly what I wanted to do. They made a game or bird preserve out of it. Today there are many types of seabirds that use this new barrier island to nest, including my terns.

An interesting point is that soon after the State decided to reserve Deveaux Bank for the people of South Carolina, an attorney from Charleston tried to buy it from me. This told me that if you persist long enough, there is no telling what you can get done. I guess my name was attached to Deveaux Bank so that he thought I owned it. As far as I know, I have not gotten any credit for forcing Deveaux Bank to be used as a bird sanctuary. But the story I just mentioned is true.

An article on Deveaux Bank by South Carolina Department of Natural Resources that I found on the internet lists the following birds that nest there. They are: brown pelican, least tern, royal tern, black skimmer, gull-billed tern, sandwich tern, and common tern. Also on the list are: laughing gull, Wilson's plover, American oystercatcher, willet, great egret, snowy egret, tricolored heron, and ibis. I am familiar with most of these birds, but it seems impossible that this many birds could all nest on Deveaux Bank. But I am proud that my birds have their own place to nest.

My daughter, while vacationing on Edisto Beach, once counted 85 pelicans flying in a row back to Deveaux Bank. We live in Store Creek, and the laughing gulls are constantly making their loud noises around our dock. It appears that they are laughing at us for working so hard and they do nothing but pick up scraps found floating on the creek as a result of leftovers from some shark not finishing the meal he killed.

It is hard to look out over Store Creek without seeing some birds. This morning a very large great blue heron landed on one of the piling on our dock and stayed there for a long time preening himself. He put on a show for us, stretching out to show us how big he was and how beautiful he was in all his glory. As a sideline, herons and egrets nest in trees on some isolated marsh islands. These nesting areas are often referred to as colonies.

Those of us who live in the local coastal area should be thankful for Deveaux Bank as it provides a place for all these birds to nest. I could write a whole book just on what I have observed the birds of Deveaux Bank doing. Even though ospreys and bald eagles do not nest on Deveaux Bank, they are frequent visitors to our Store Creek. A whole book could be written about these two awesome birds.

It is one thing to read about all the birds on Deveaux Bank but another thing to actually see them in action. As I have already related, from time to time as I passed Deveaux Bank through the deep channel that is between it and Botany Bay Island, I would stop and watch the baby pelicans in pools of water.They seemed to run across the water, trying to lift off on their own wings. As I watched, some actually made it into the air. If they did not make it, the young pelicans would go back and try again until they made it into flight.

Sometimes I took the ocean side of Deveaux Bank and once saw hundreds of young seagulls being herded into the water by their parents. During my time of going back and forth to Rockville to the summer sailboat races, Deveaux Bank grew in size, and more and more birds came to make their nests. When I first was aware of the birds on Deveaux Bank, there were only pelicans and gulls nesting on the Bank. There may have been others, but I did not observe them at the time. My initial experience with Deveaux Bank was in the early 1950s as a teenager.

Here is how Deveaux Bank was built to about two miles by two miles with a small bay in the back facing inland. At low tide the beach's sand gets dry. The wind picks up this dry sand, and when it hits beach grass or anything solid, it drops the sand, and a sand dune begins. In a short time, you have a sizeable barrier island. Hurricane David in the 1980s almost destroyed it, but the wind and sand process rebuilt it. When the plantation owners began to build tall two-story beach houses, I guess they failed to realize that all barrier islands were subject to the same fate as Deveaux Bank. If they knew this, it would have been wiser to build small cottages to use to eat and sleep so their investment would be expendable when Mother Nature in all her fury came calling.

I presented this chapter because the three barrier islands protecting the sea island named Edisto Island were built the same way as Deveaux Bank is continuously being built. If the ocean allows it one day, Deveaux Bank may be as big as Edisto Beach. Or one day a great hurricane may level Deveaux Bank to just another sandbar that only comes out of the water at low tide.

Sadly, Edingsville experienced the fury of several storms and was reduced to a narrow strip of land. If the ocean keeps moving this small strip of land inland, it will be no more when its sand is pushed over into Frampton Creek.

Ode to Edingsville

Oh, Edingville, where have you gone?

We miss your stately houses looking out to sea.

What sin did you commit to allow the sea and wind to punish you so badly?

Oh, Edingsville we miss you so!

Your name will go down in history as a lovely place to let down your hair and lift up your voice in glee.

The birds flew away because they knew that a storm was coming as the large waves built out to sea.

Oh, Edingsville, did you not know that houses built on sand could not stand a raging sea.

Rolling, rolling, rolling, came the sea, with little waves that came on the beach, getting larger and larger as the sea began to show her strength.

Oh, Edingsville, where did you take your children when you saw the dark clouds bringing the storm ashore?

Cry, cry for your shining white summer houses as the storm takes them away.

Oh, Edingsville, will there ever be another like you, a place to dance and play to sunrise?

Crash, crash was the sound from afar as we heard the storm tearing our wonderful Edingsville away.

Oh, Edingsville, if only you were built on sound ground as the plantation houses were built.

The sand dunes that seem forever came sliding down into the sea as the storm water got deeper and deeper, rushing forward.

Oh, Edingsville, you provided a place safe from swamp fever for a few years, but now you are gone, and we long for thee.

The storm is now gone, the welcoming beach houses are gone too. What an empty feeling I have for the loss of thee.

Oh, Edingsville, I can now only read about you and let my mind dream of a place like you.

Because of this book, you will be remembered for years to come.

But, oh, Edingsville, I can still look acrossJeremy Inlet and dream of all that happened there.

Let us write and sing a song of Edingsville that will fill our hearts of this once wonderful place!

Oh, Edingsville, We Cry for Thee!

The answer to the question of how we should live: (Jesus Christ speaking.)

"But he answered and said, It is written, Man shall not live by bread alone, but by every word that proceedeth out of the mouth of God." - **Matthew 4:4 KJV**

In other words, you should live by every word written in the Bible (God's Holy Words).

This is a picture of Sam Lybrand and his wife, Joyce. Sam did the research and Joyce did the editing.

Made in the USA
Columbia, SC
22 May 2023

16655906R00055